The
Beauty
of
Imperfection

Photos and Memories of France
ca 1988-1999
Cathy LW Gorgensen

First edition April 2023
Editor: Amy M. Le
Jacket design by Cathy LW Gorgensen and Virginia McKevitt

Manufactured in the United States of America

Hardcover ISBN: 979-8-9869102-5-3
Paperback ISBN: 979-8-9850905-2-9
EBook ISBN: 979-8-9875646-4-6

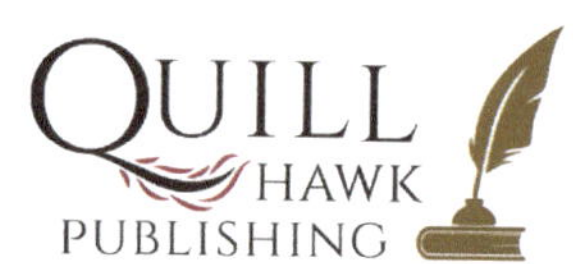

For My Husband Bill
Thank you for your unconditional love and support
I Love You

"Photography is an art of teleporting the past into the future." –Mehmet Murat ildan (1965), Writer

In 1989 my husband Bill and I moved to a small town in France called La Varenne-Saint-Hilaire, a suburb southeast of Paris. Before leaving the States, Bill gifted me with a Nikon N2020 35mm film camera. We moved into a lovely home, three houses up from the Marne River that flows nearby. I loaded up my backpack with water, lots of film, and the desire to explore our new location. I spent hours in my darkroom developing my photos while Chewy, our cat, waited outside the door.

Living in France was truly magical. The things those old buildings have seen and heard. Too bad they can't talk. Getting lost was typically unfortunate for anyone but not for me in Paris. I wandered endlessly and stumbled upon something new every time. Maybe because I knew this was not our permanent home, it made every day much more special.

A feeling of awe would wash over me as I walked down an alleyway or some random cobblestone street as I let my mind wander and imagined some of the greatest minds ever had walked these same streets.

Of course, we explored the obligatory things one must see and do—Versailles, Provence, Chantilly, etc. But we also visited towns we had never heard of, or someone from work would tell us, "You must see this place," and off we'd go. Sometimes a coin had to be flipped to see if we went left or right. We were never disappointed. It was like discovering something new—the sights, smells, and sounds different from one another—a photographer's paradise.

Those were beautiful days that I would never forget; days spent exploring and appreciating the beauty of life all around me through my lens—capturing memories that will last forever in my mind's eye.

The photos in this book are just some of the stories I wanted to share. Maybe they'll remind you of vacations taken, that first kiss, or when you walked down those same cobblestone streets or watched the sunset while drinking an espresso at a sidewalk cafe. Perhaps they'll inspire you to get out more and explore the world around you.

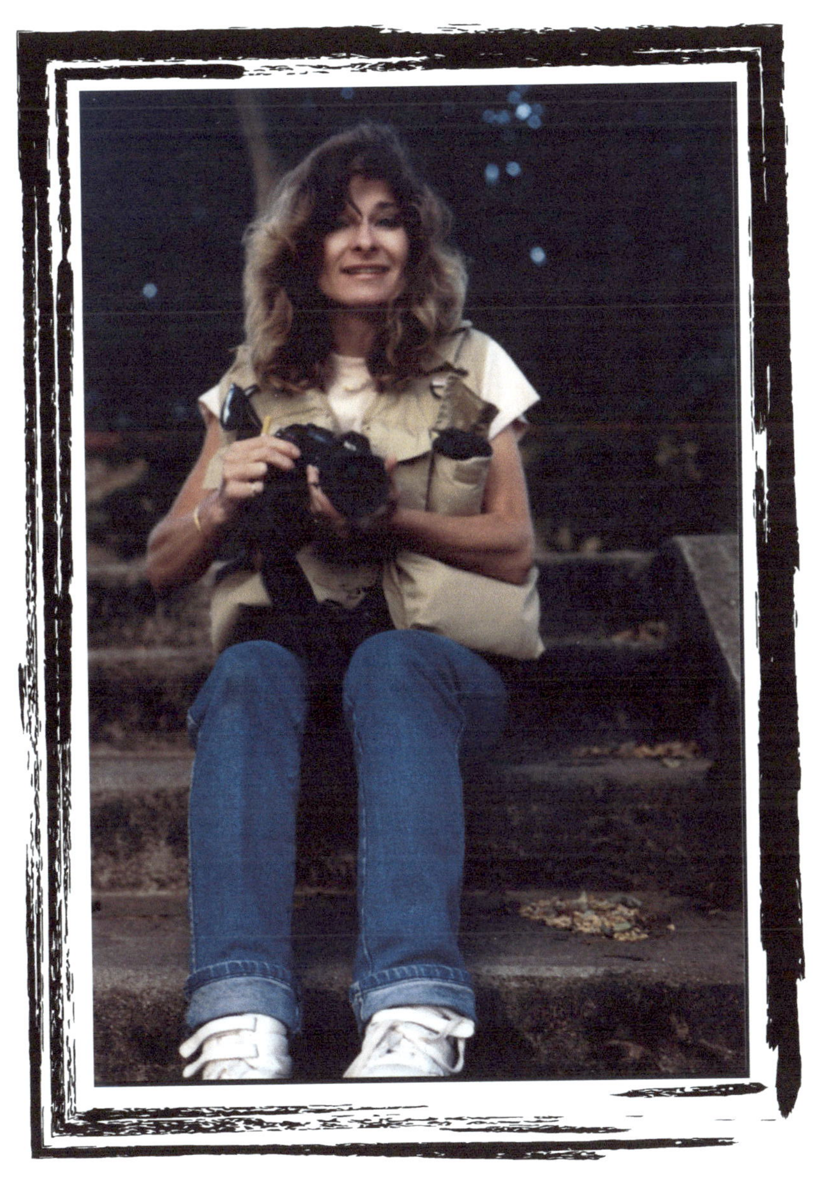

Photo of Cathy LW Gorgensen by Carol Lema, Lavarenne, France ca 1989-1992

Through the lens, one's true nature can emerge, capturing moments that reflect personal perspectives, passions, and emotions. The photos we take reveal the essence of who we are, unveiling hidden desires, creativity, and connections to the world around us, offering glimpses into the depths of our souls.

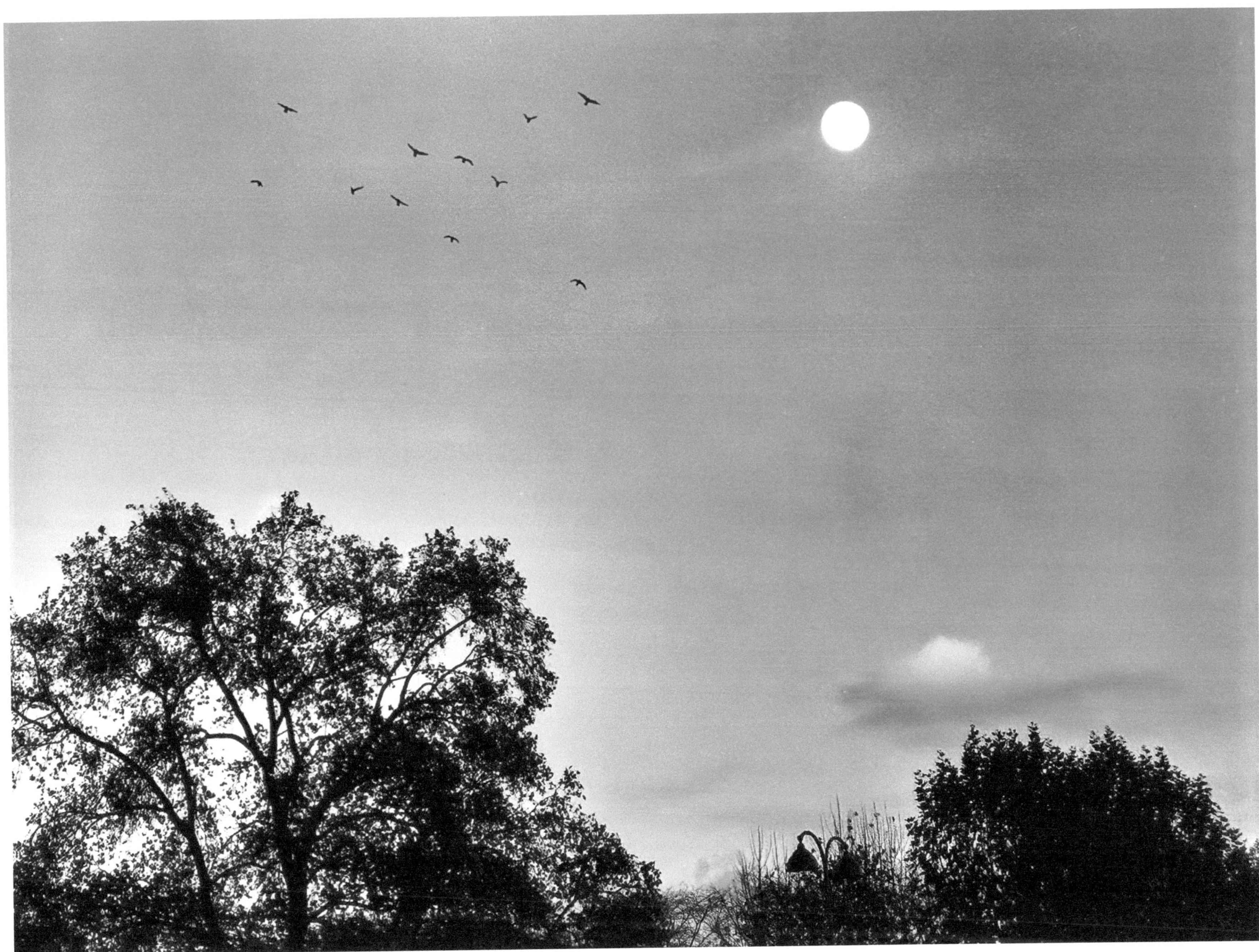

"Our lives are stories, and the stories we have to give to each other are the most important. No one has a story too small, and all are of equal stature. We each tell them in different ways, through different mediums - and if we care about each other, we'll take the time to listen."

-Charles de Lint (1951), Canadian Author

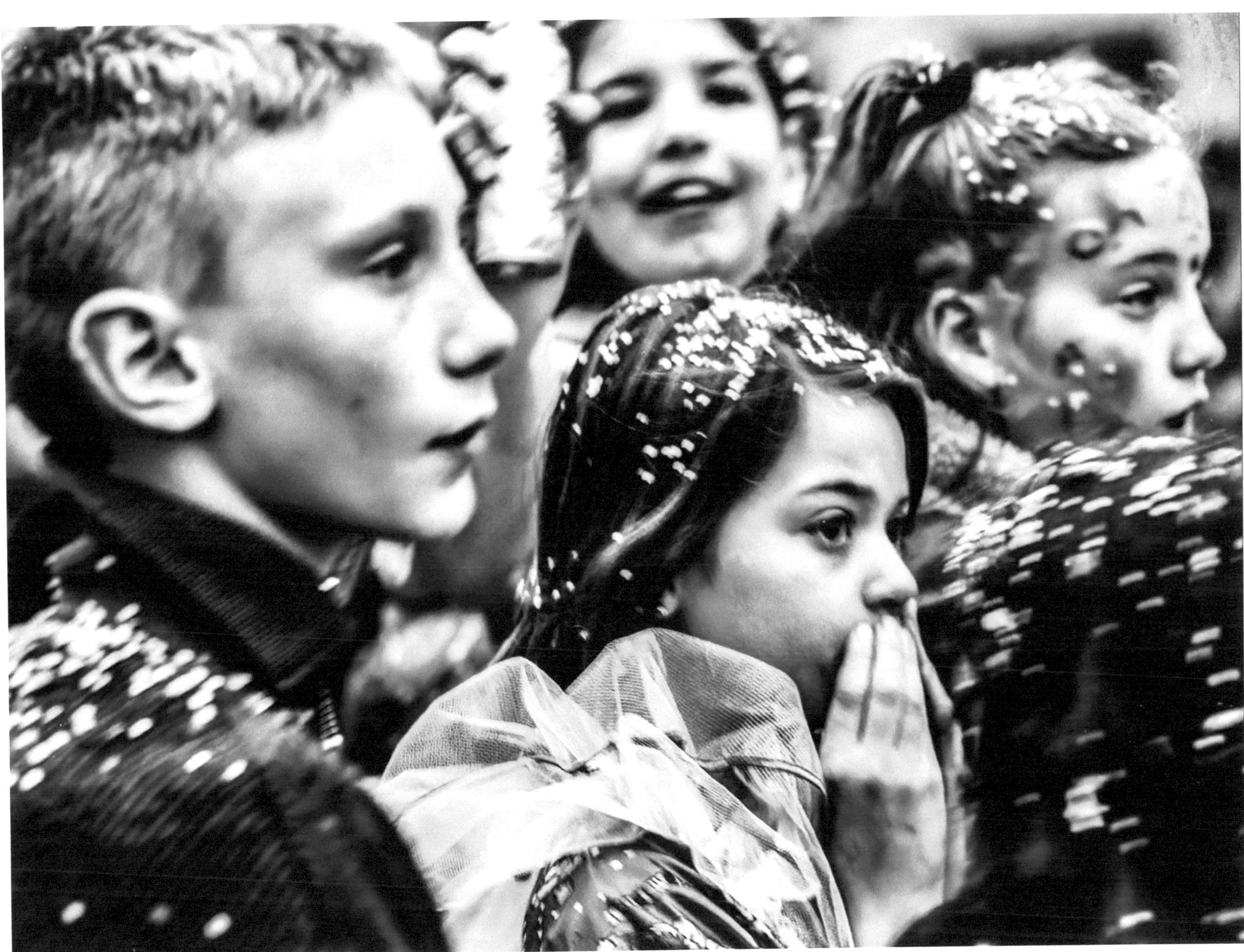

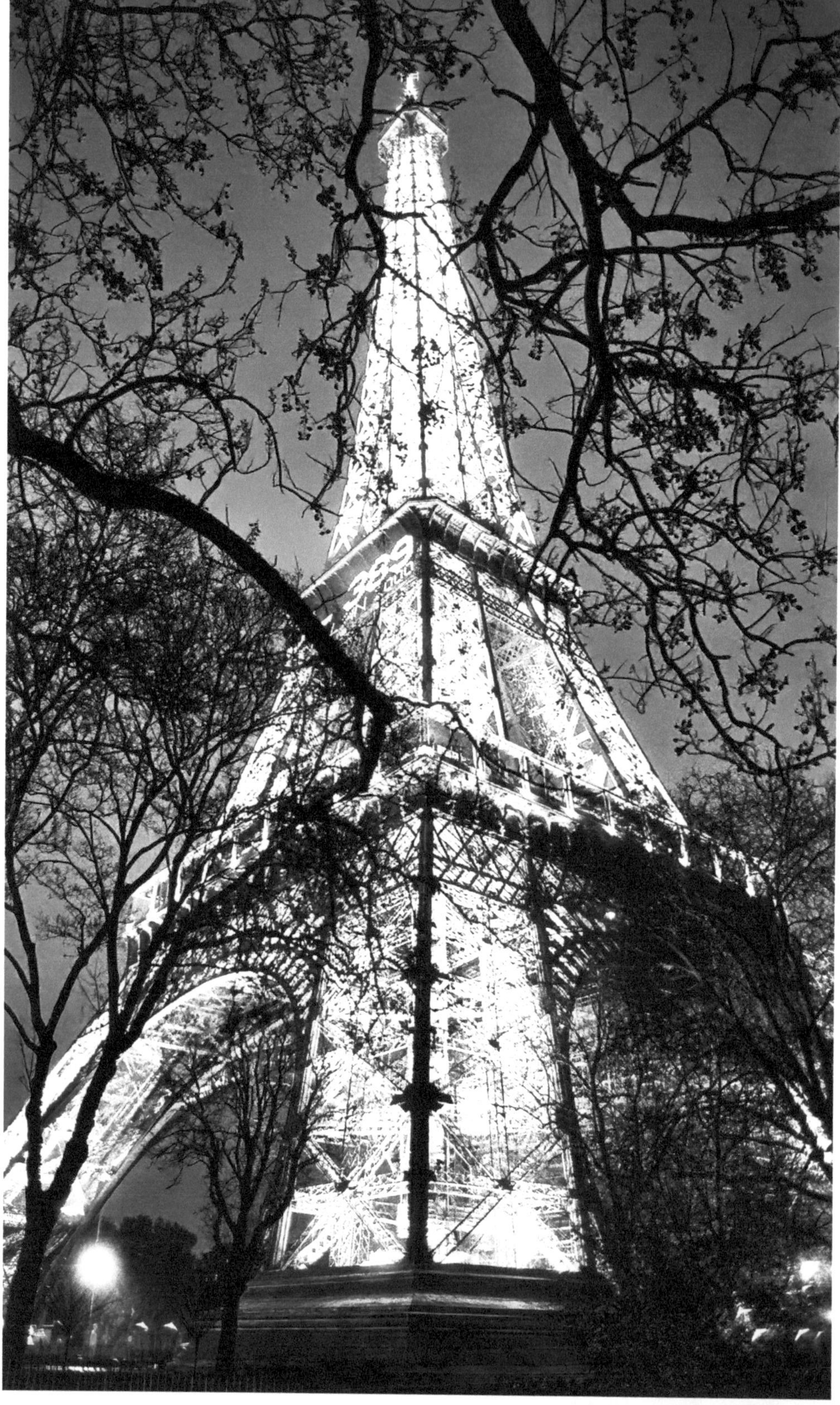

Even after multiple visits, it's amazing how the Eiffel Tower continues to leave a lasting impression on you. Its stunning architecture has the power to inspire.

"Can one think that because we are engineers, beauty does not preoccupy us or that we do not try to build beautiful, as well as solid and long-lasting structures? Aren't the genuine functions of strength always in keeping with unwritten conditions of harmony? Besides, there is an attraction, a special charm in the colossal to which ordinary theories of art do not apply."
–Gustave Eiffel (1832-1923), whose company designed and built the Eiffel Tower

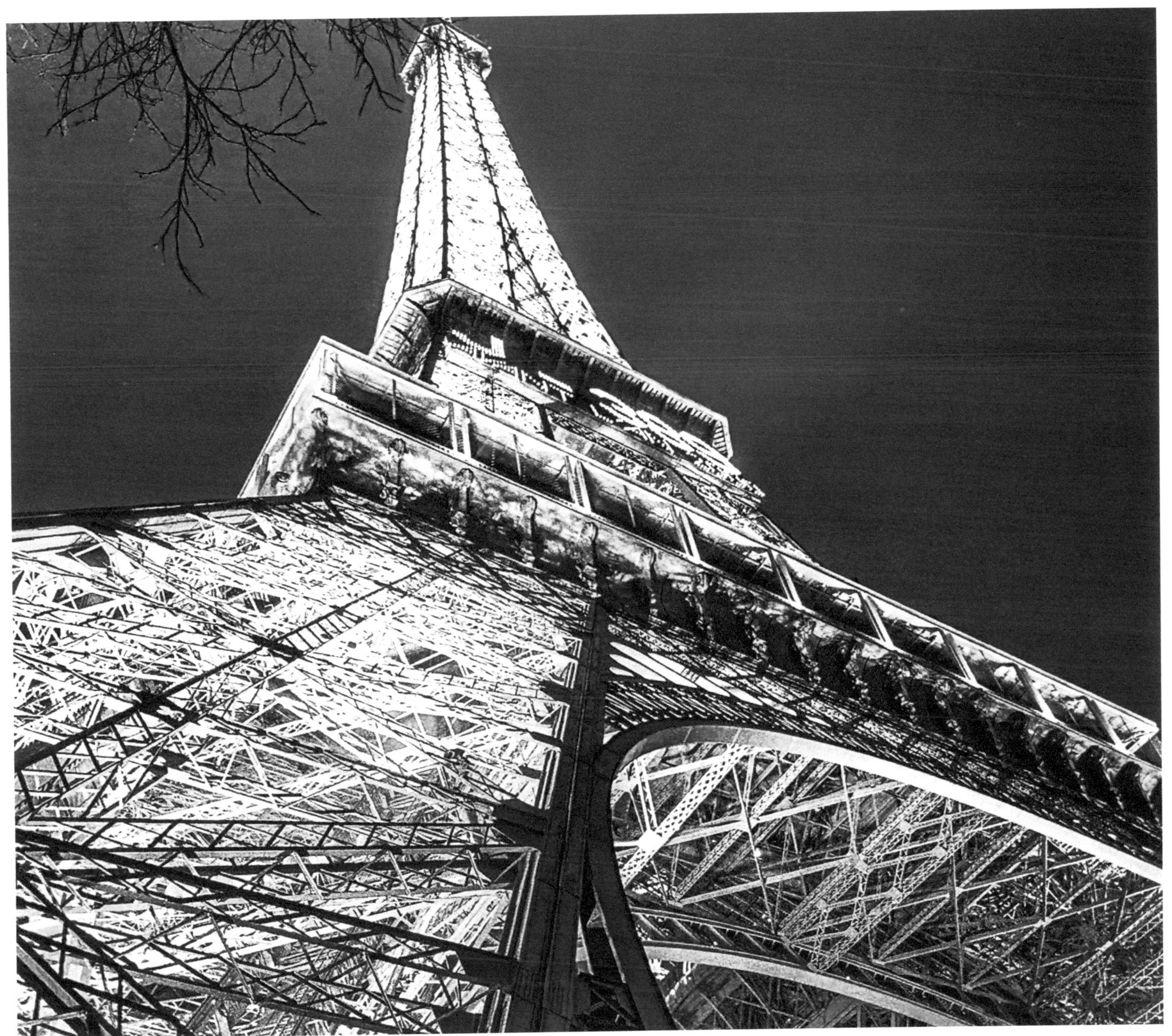

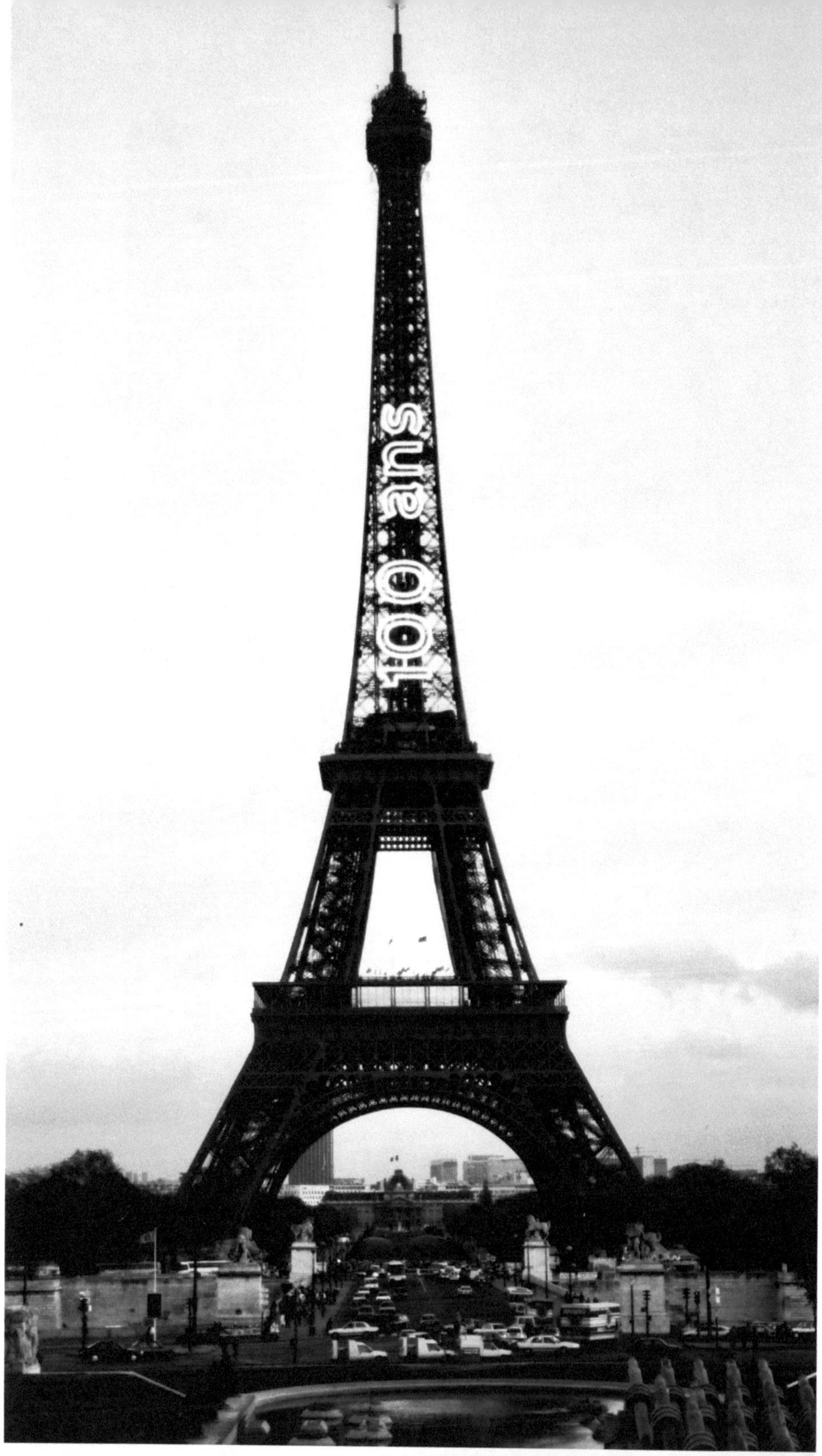

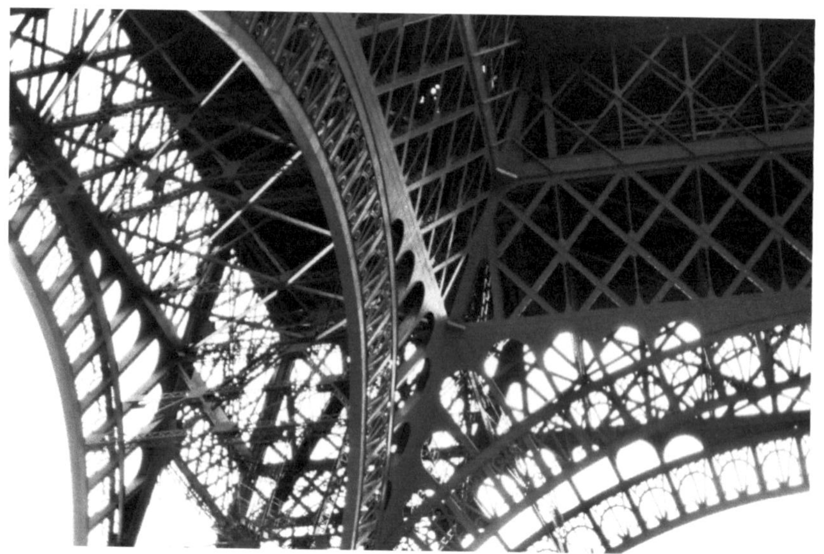

Locally nicknamed "La dame de fer" (French for "Iron Lady"), it was constructed from 1887 to 1889 as the centerpiece of the 1889 Worlds Fair.

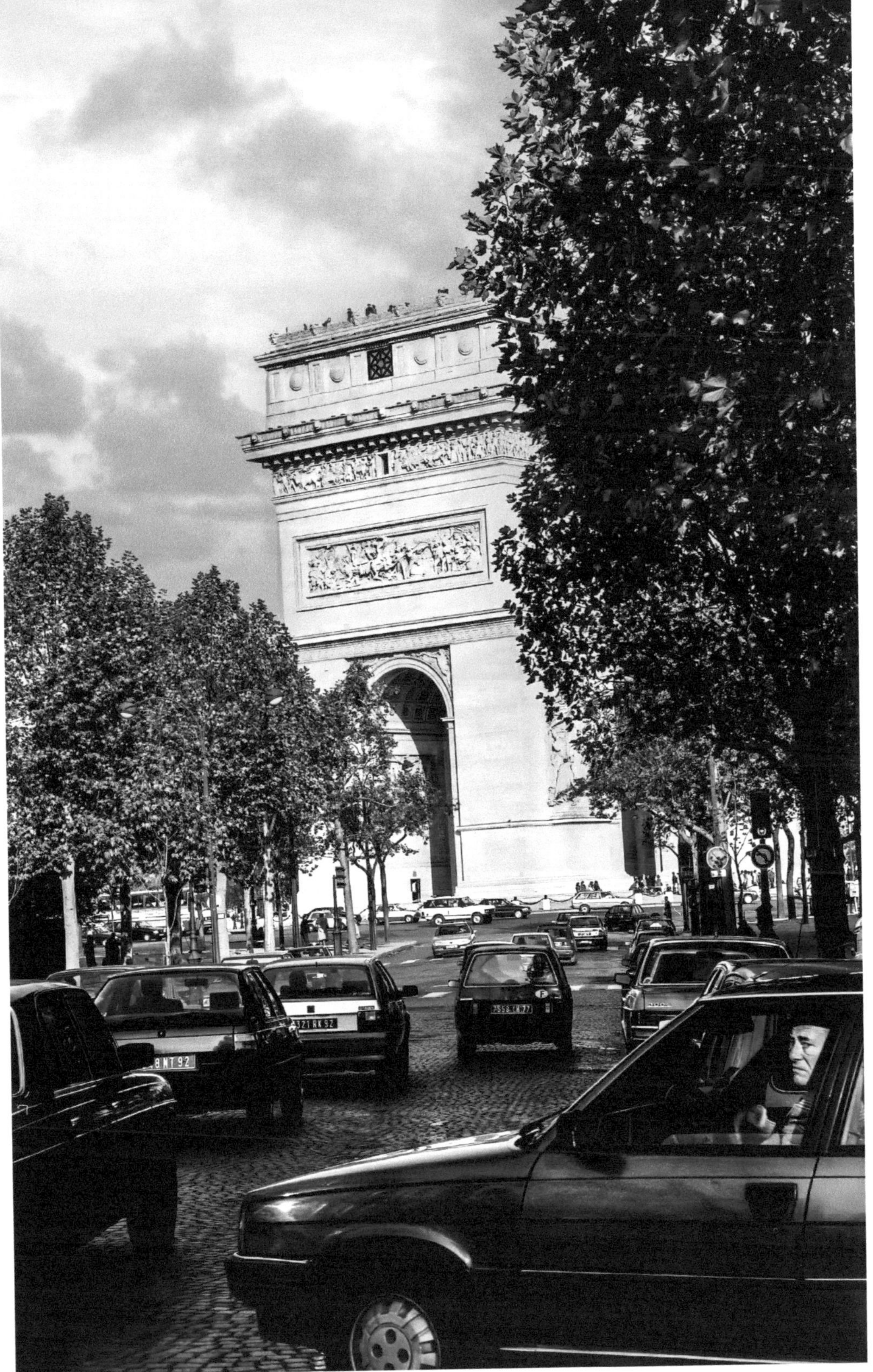

"You don't make a photograph just with a camera. You bring to the act of photography all the pictures you have seen, the books you have read, the music you have heard, the people you have loved."

–Ansel Adams (1902-1984), American landscape photographer and environmentalist

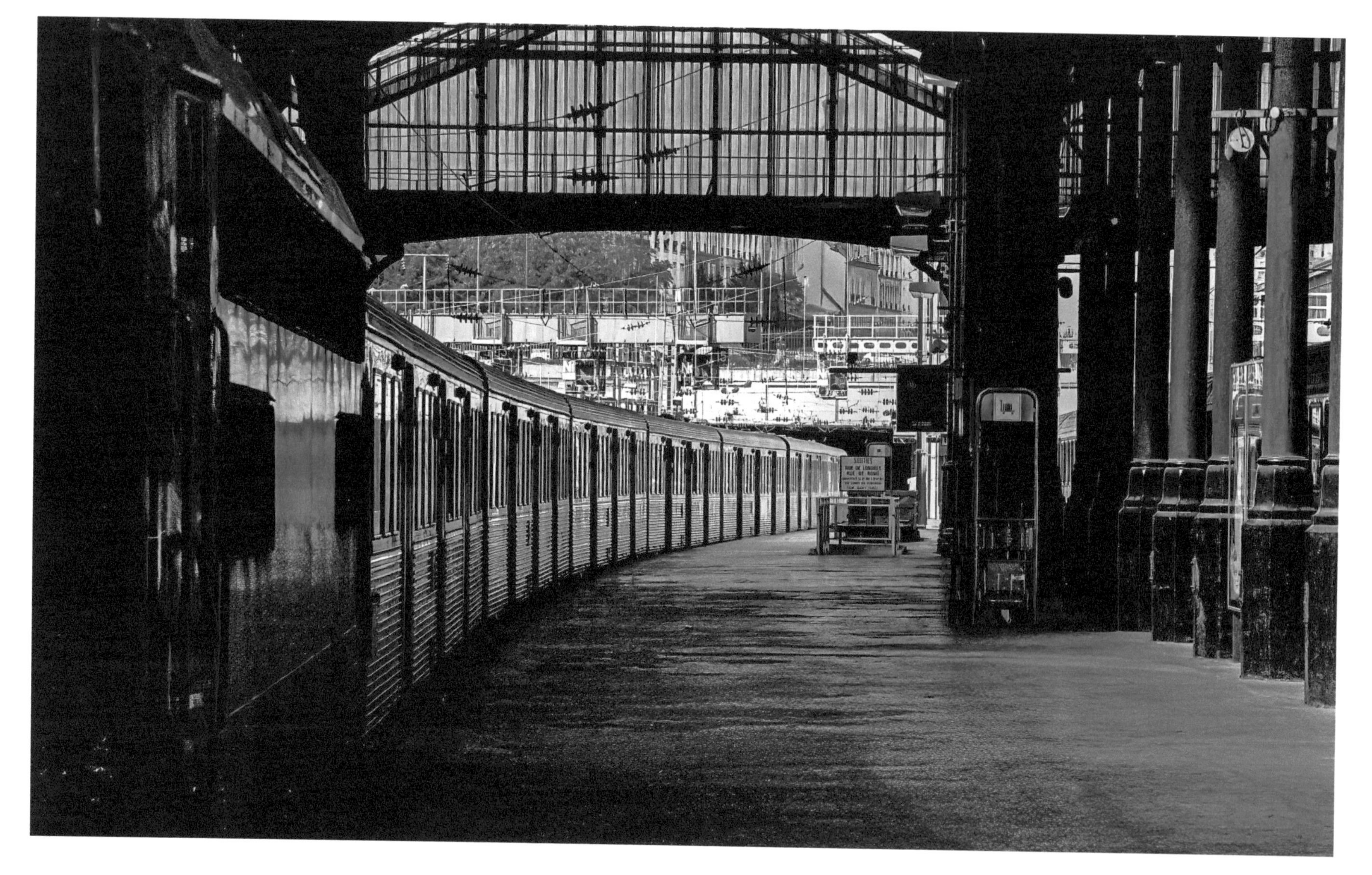

Gare Saint-Lazare (English: St Lazarus station), officially Paris-Saint-Lazare, is one of the seven large mainline railway stations in Paris, France.

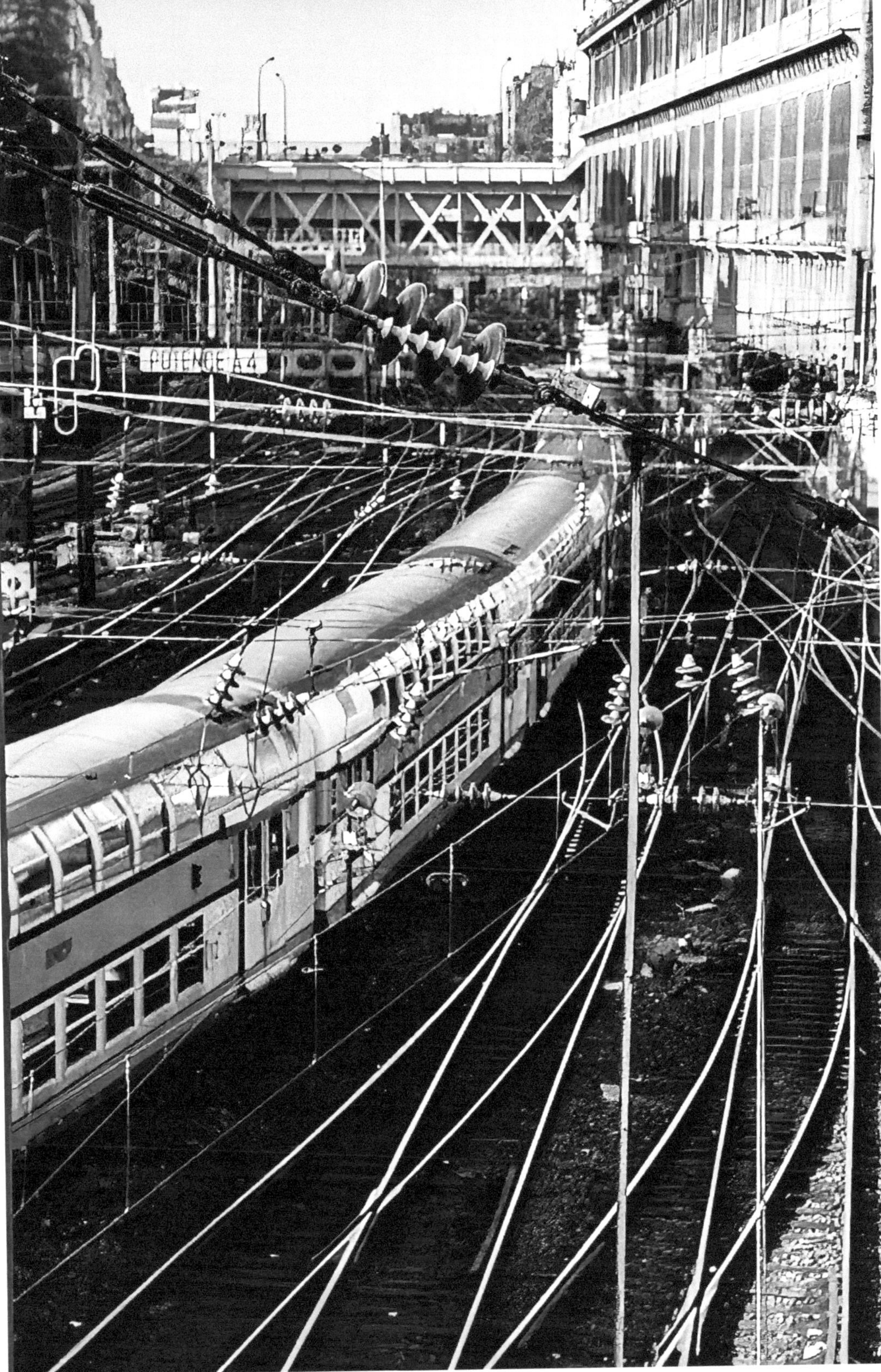

"Paris is the city in which one loves to live. Sometimes I think this is because it is the only city in the world where you can step out of a railway station—the Gare d'Orsay—and see, simultaneously, the chief enchantments: the Seine with its bridges and bookstalls, the Louvre, Notre Dame, the Tuileries Gardens, the Place de la Concorde, the beginning of the Champs Elysees—nearly everything except the Luxembourg Gardens and the Palais Royal. But what other city offers as much as you leave a train?"
—Margaret Anderson (1886-1973),
American author & editor

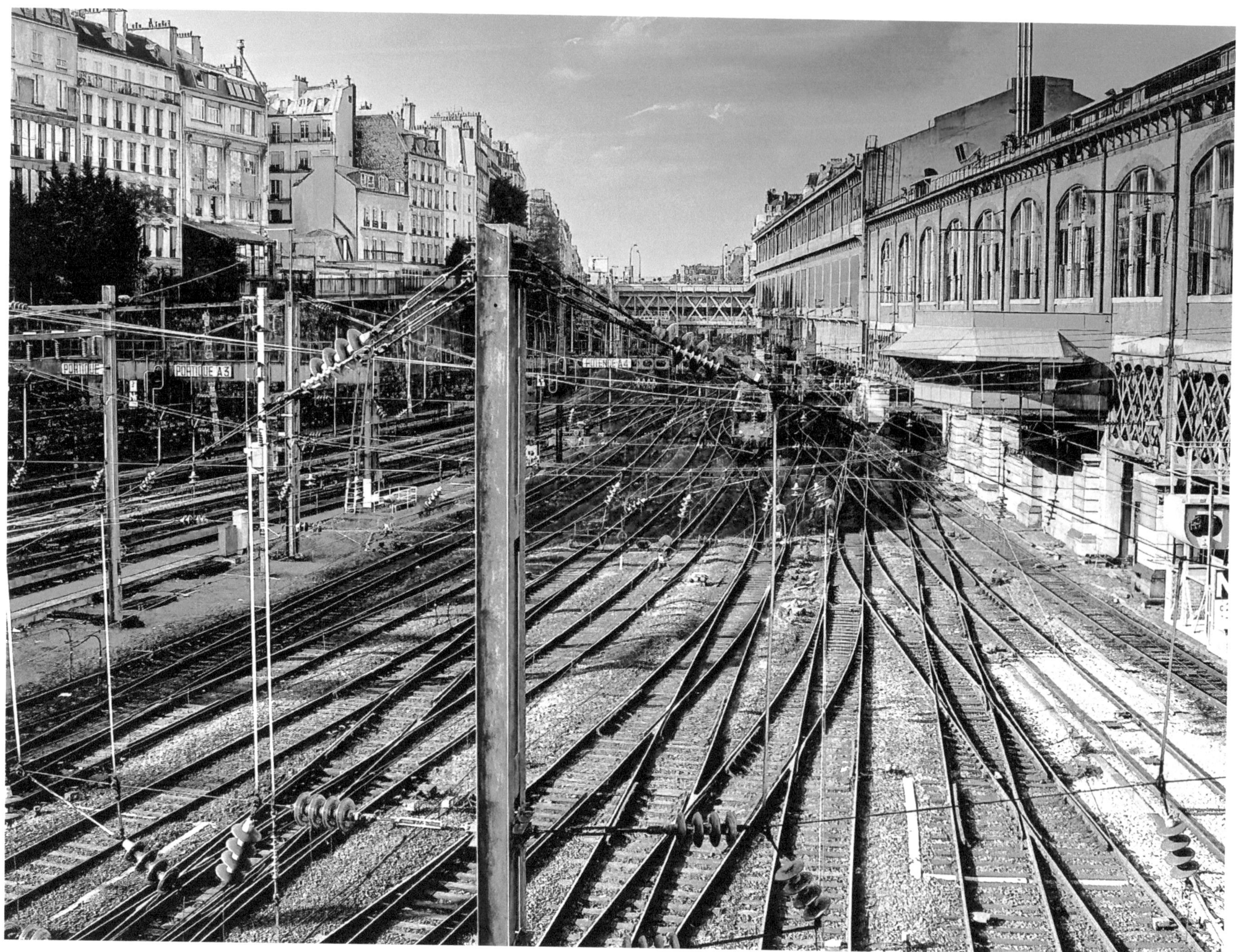

PORTIQUE
PORTIQUE A3
PORTIQUE A4

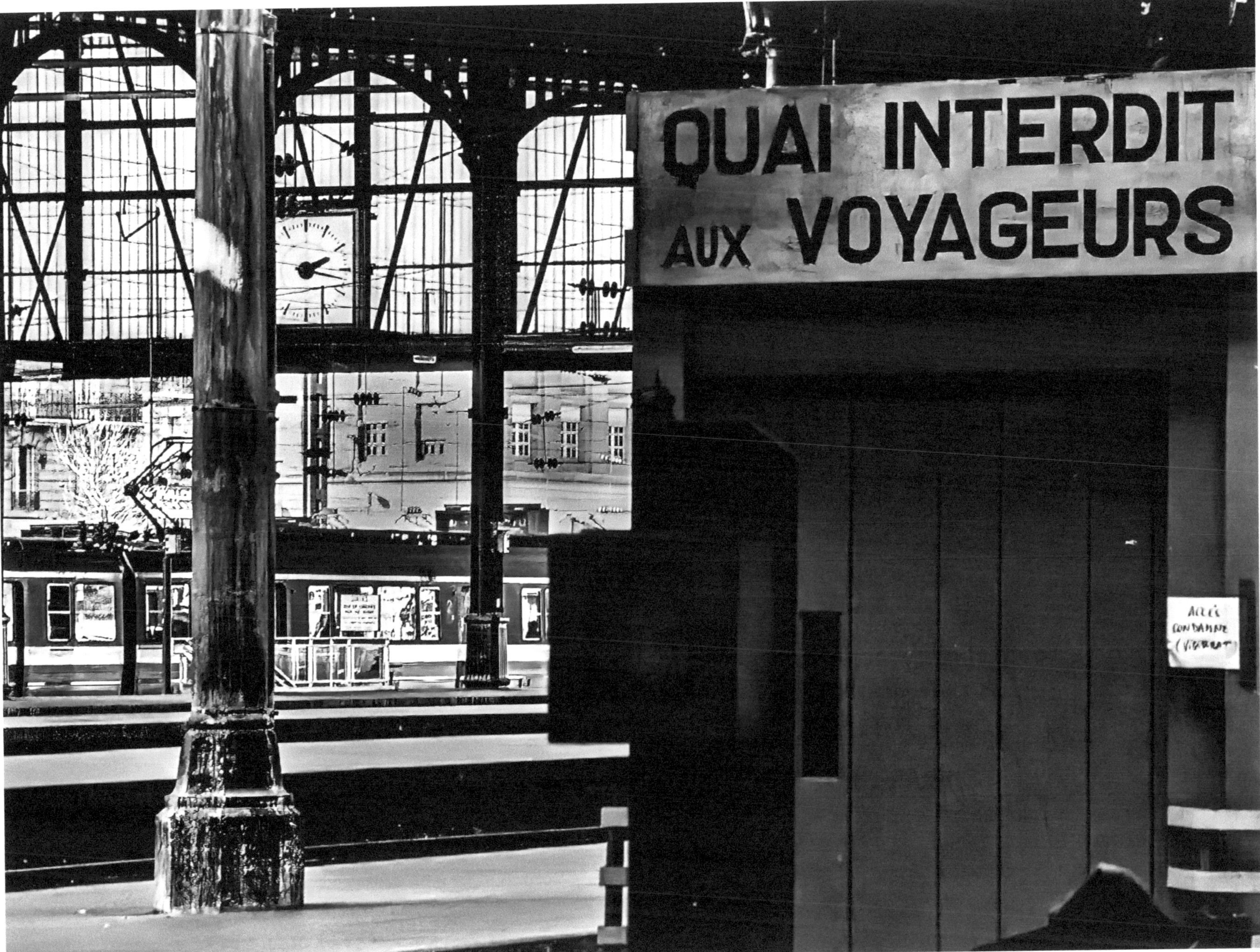

QUAI INTERDIT
AUX VOYAGEURS
ACCÈS
CONDAMNÉ
(VIBERT)

"Sharpness is a bourgeois concept."
-Henri Cartier-Bresson (1908-2004),
Photographer and painter

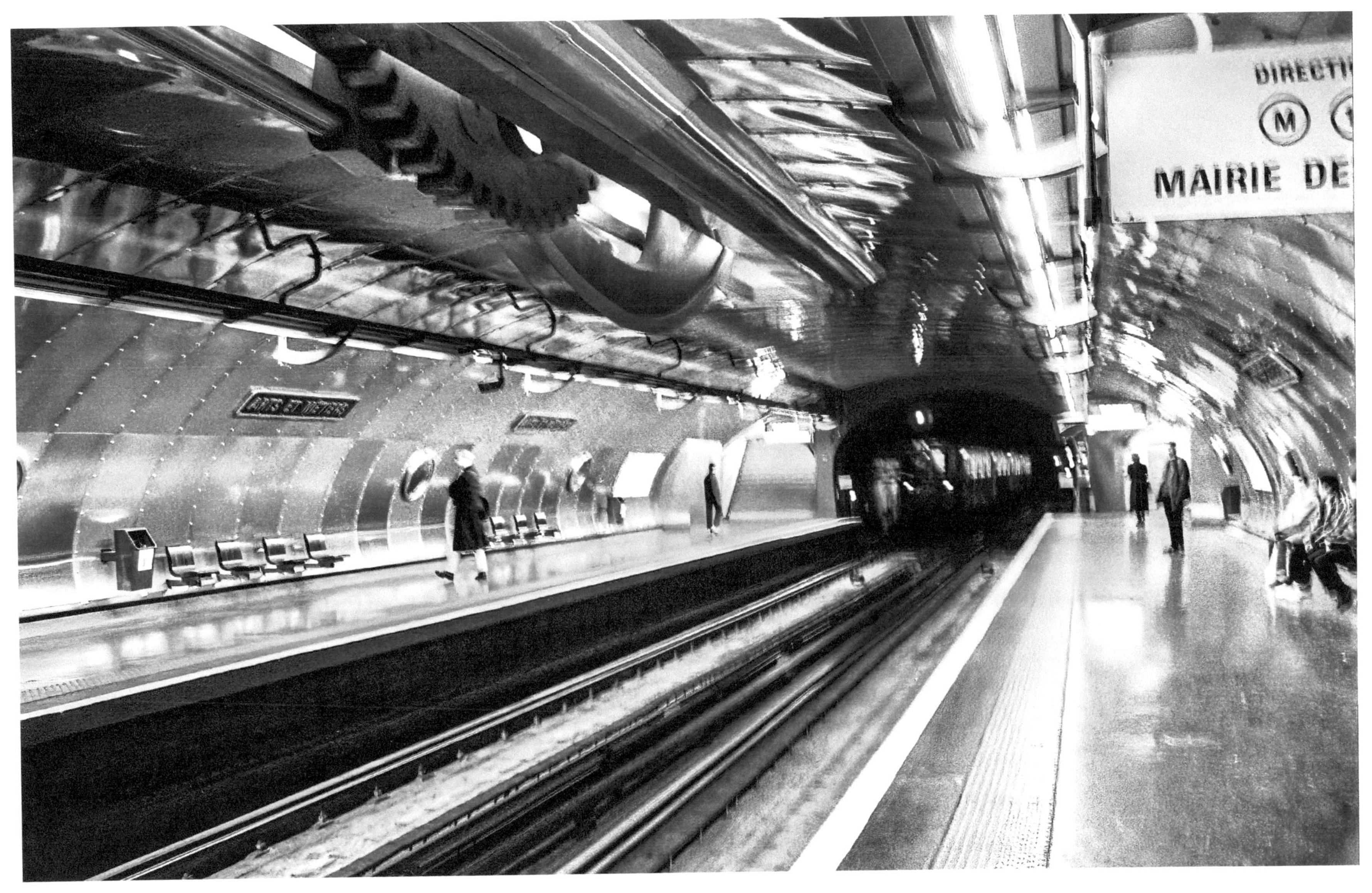

ARTS ET MÉTIERS METRO is a station on Line 3 and Line 11 of the Paris Métro and located in the 3rd arrondissement of Paris; it gives commuters access to the musée des Arts et Métiers situated at 60 rue Réaumur. The museum is as beautiful and extraordinary as this metro.

The Church of Saint-Germain-l'Auxerrois is a Roman Catholic church in the First Arrondissement of Paris, situated at 2 Place du Louvre, directly across from the Louvre Palace. First built in the 7th century, it has seen many renovations. When the Louvre was still a royal palace, this church was the royal parish church. Charles V of the House of Valois turned the fortress of the Louvre into a royal residence during the 1300s. The tower on the left belongs to the town hall that serves the 1st arrondissement.

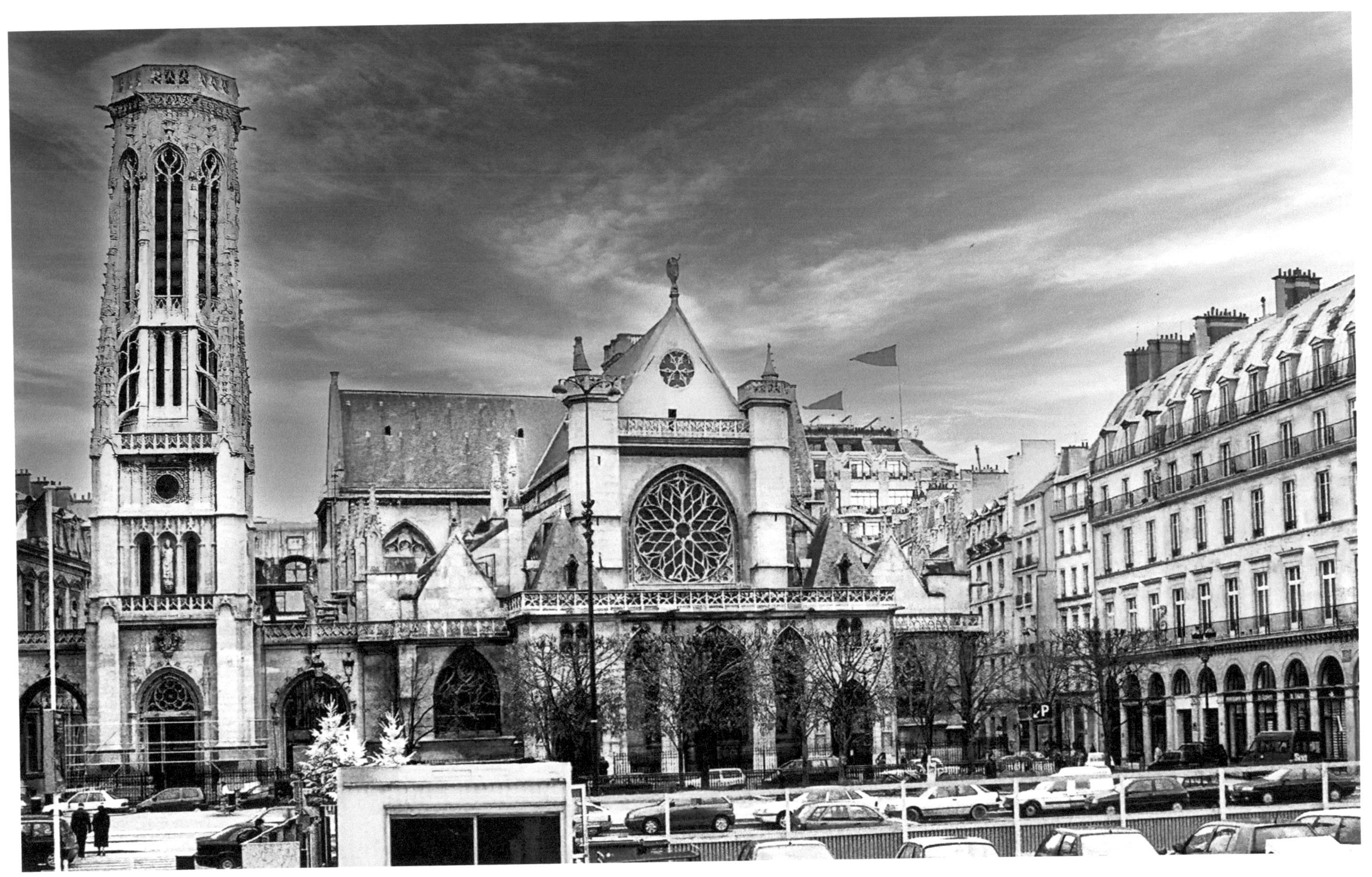

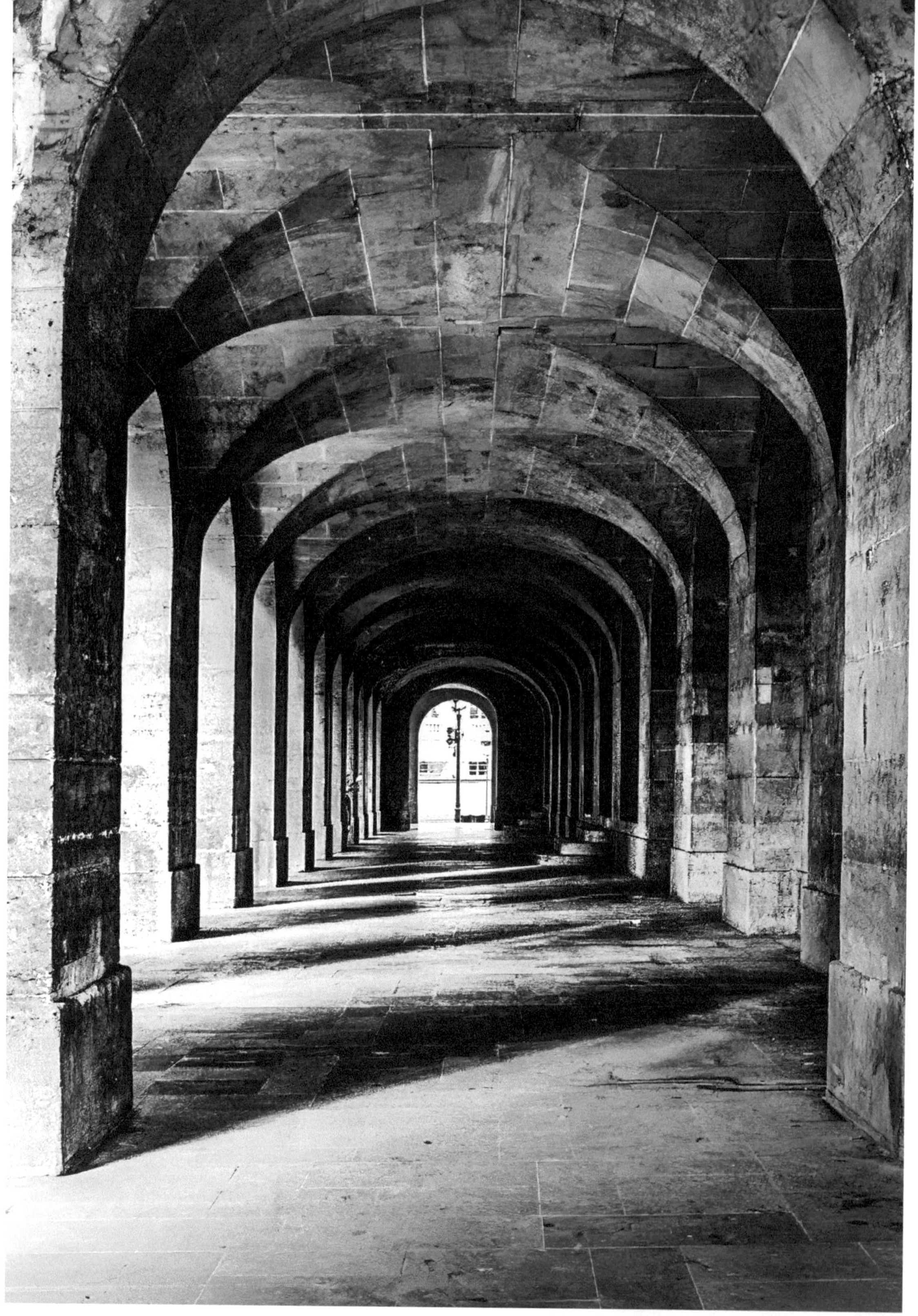

In Paris, it was impossible not to be emotionally moved. Walking anywhere sometimes felt like I was going back in time. The thought of being in a place so steeped in history inspired awe and wonder in equal measure.

Every street I turned down, I wondered who had walked before me, saw the same old and new buildings, sat at the same bar, ordered from the same bakery or patisserie, and sat at the same outdoor cafe.

Exploring Paris became overwhelming at times if I let it. But like anything, I eventually adapted and learned to be present, trying never to take any moment for granted.

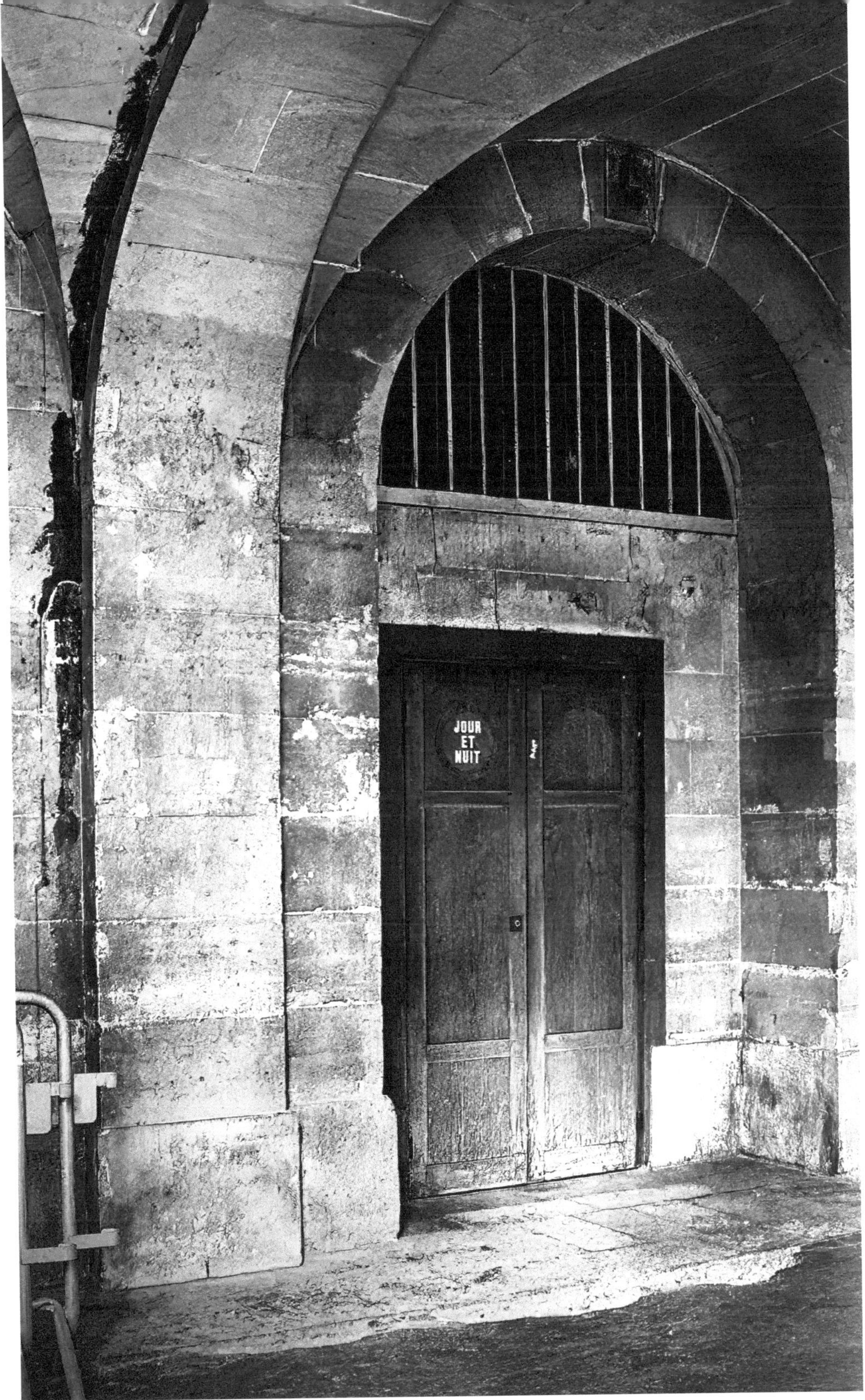

I have always been intrigued by closed doors and love capturing them on camera. My curiosity often gets the better of me, prompting me to push the door. If it opens, I am compelled to go inside and explore. But if it's locked, I accept that it wasn't meant for me to go through.

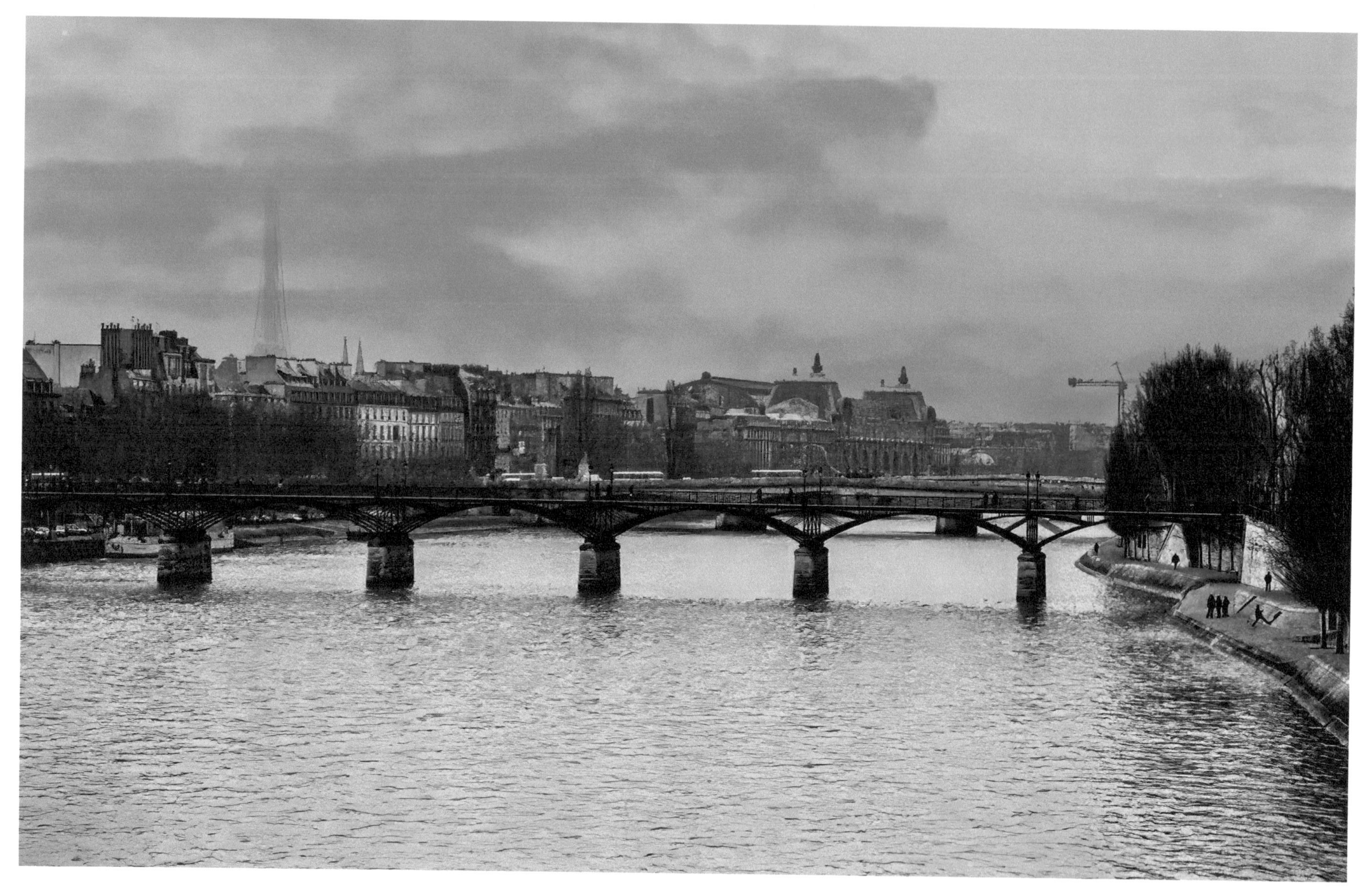

The **Pont des Arts** or **Passerelle des Arts** is a pedestrian bridge in Paris that crosses the River Seine. It links the Institut de France and the central square (cour carrée) of the Palais du Louvre (which had been termed the "Palais des Arts" under the First French Empire).

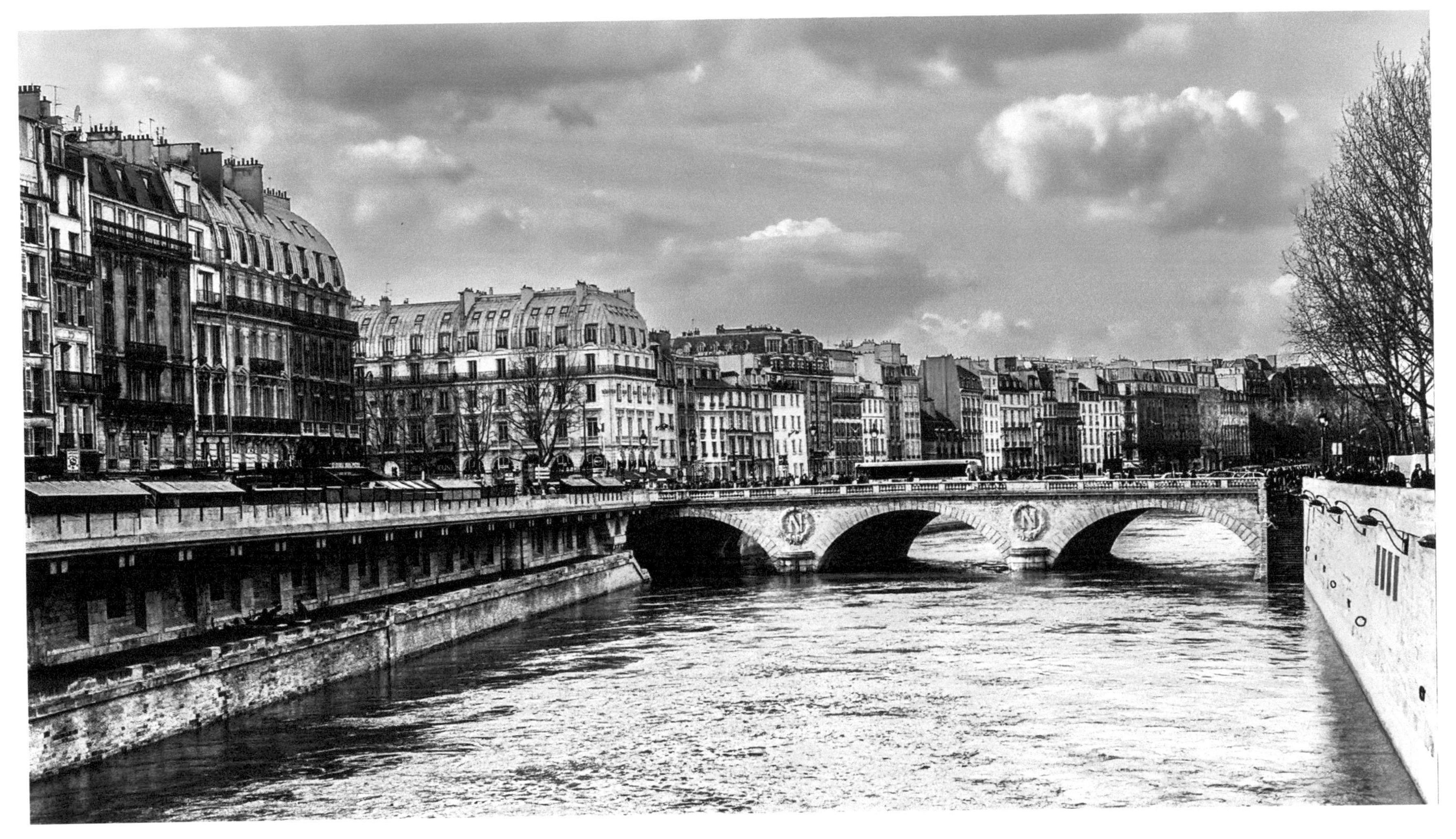

Le Pont St-Michel in Paris was *originally* known as Petit Pont-Neuf and was built between 1379 and 1387. It collapsed in 1407/08 and was rebuilt several times, with the current stone bridge constructed in 1857 during the Second Empire. The bridge connects the Palais de Justice on the Ile de la Cité to the Place Saint-Michel in the Latin Quarter and used to have houses built on it until a Royal Decree in 1786 stipulated that they be removed due to the pressure they placed on the bridge's foundations. The current bridge bears the capital letter N, the imperial insignia of Napoleon III.

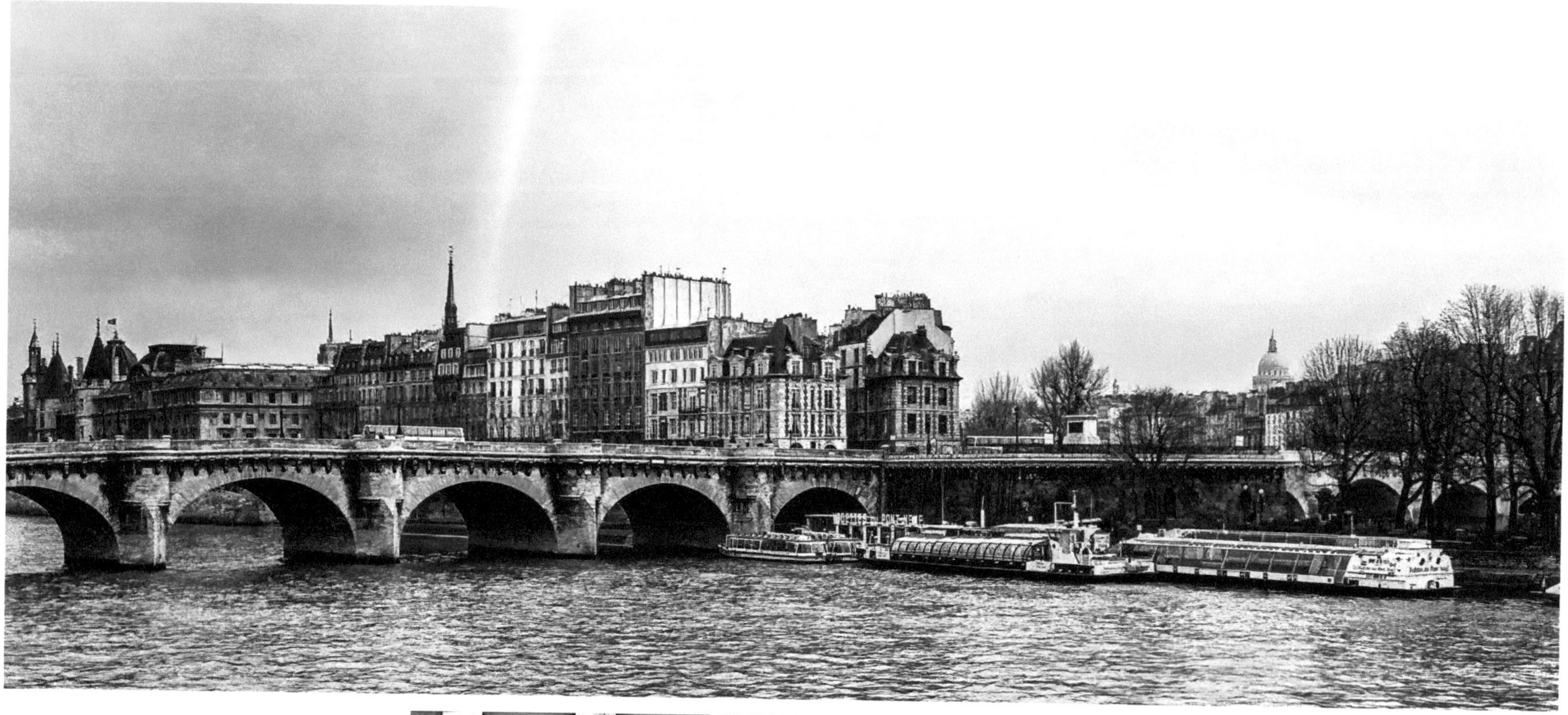

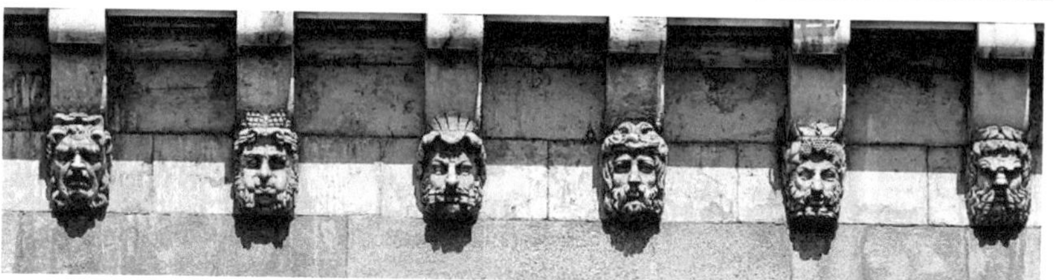

From Wikimedia Commons, the free media repository

Pont Neuf, the oldest bridge across the River Seine in Paris, was inaugurated in 1607 and is composed of two separate spans. The bridge was the first stone bridge in Paris without supporting houses. It underwent many repairs and renovations, including rebuilding seven spans and lowering the roadway. The bridge features 381 different mascarons, each representing the heads of forest and field deities, satyrs, and sylvans from ancient mythology. In 1994, a significant renovation for the Pont Neuf began, lasting 13 years, and was completed in 2007 for the 400th year anniversary of the bridge.

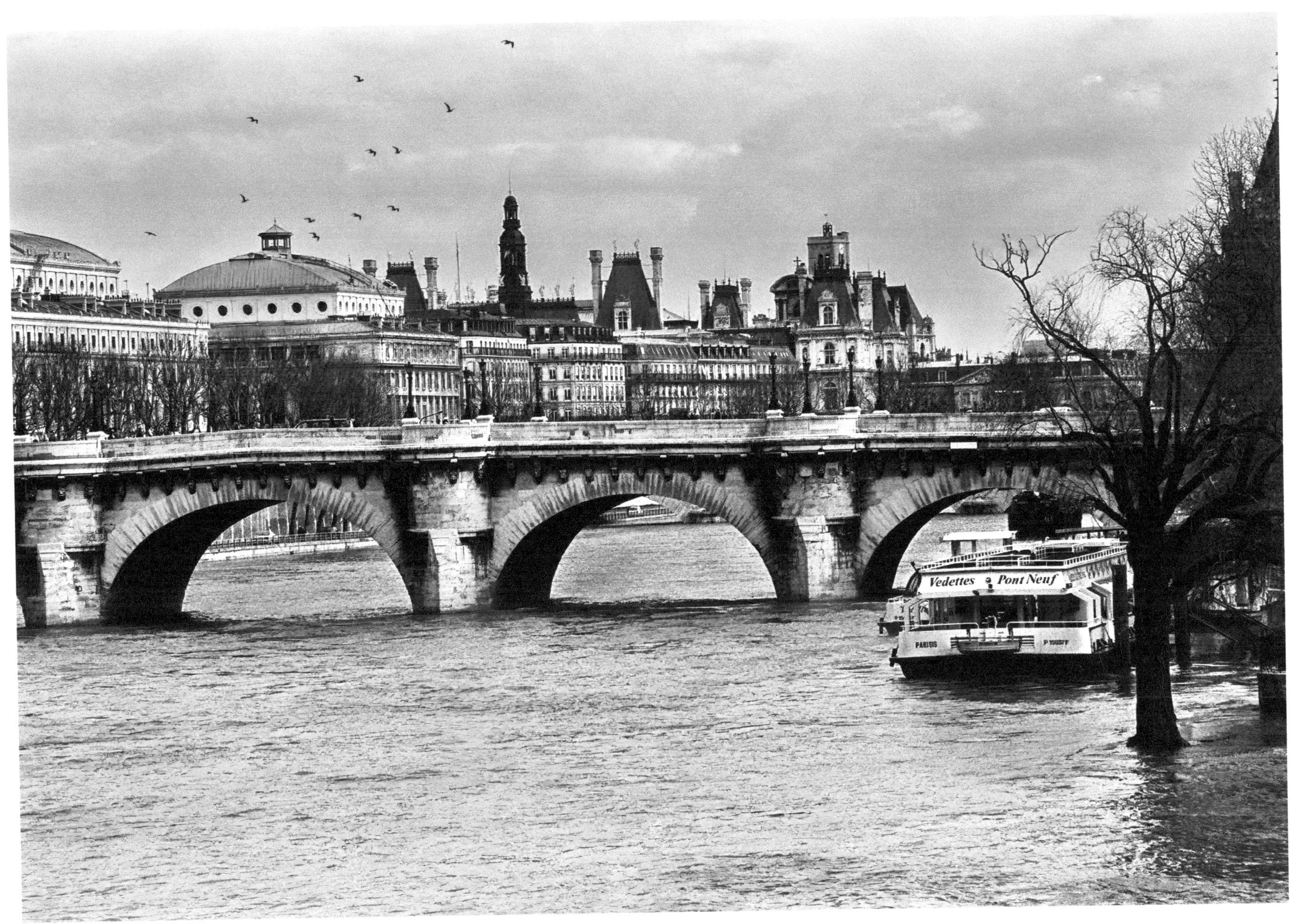

Pont Neuf

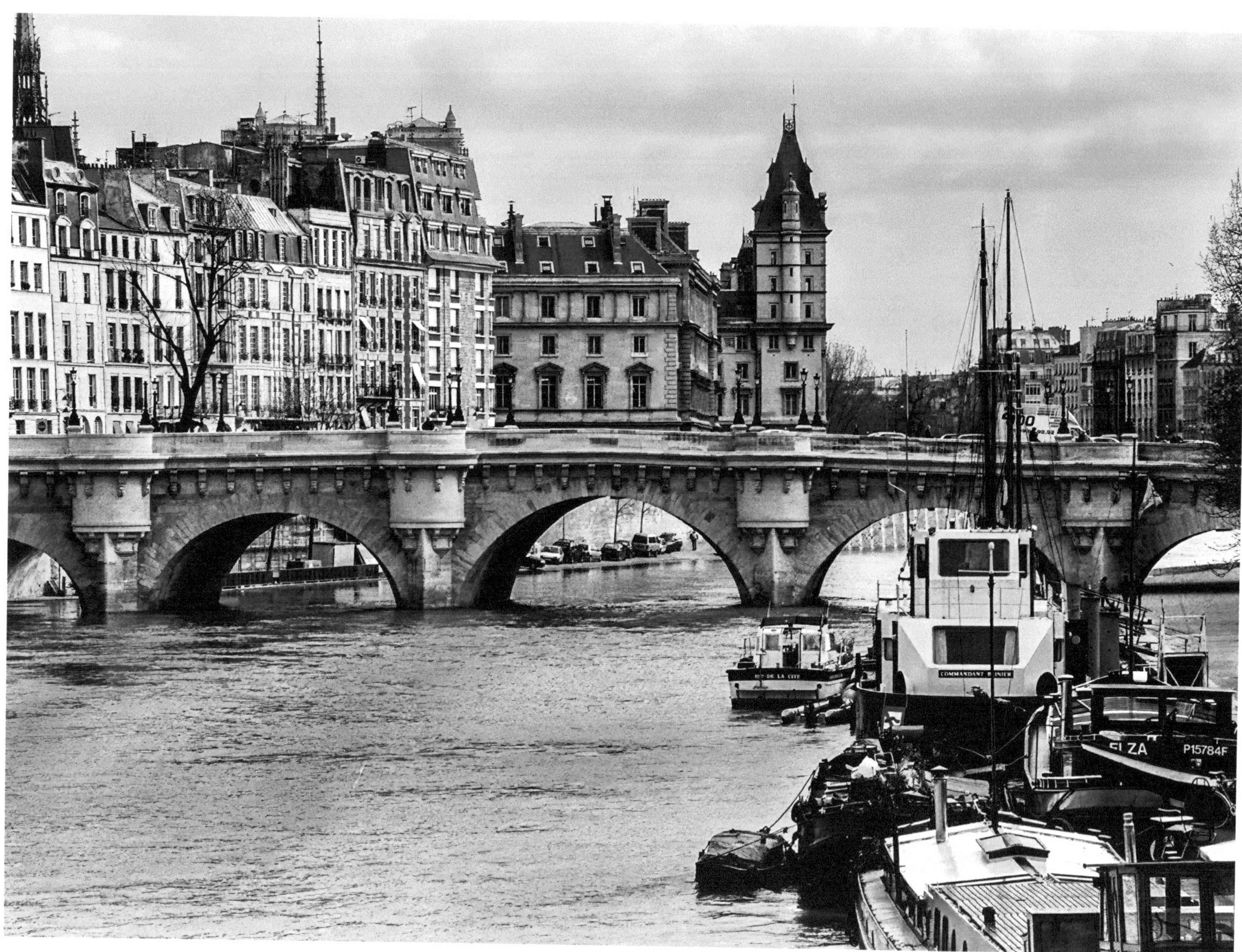

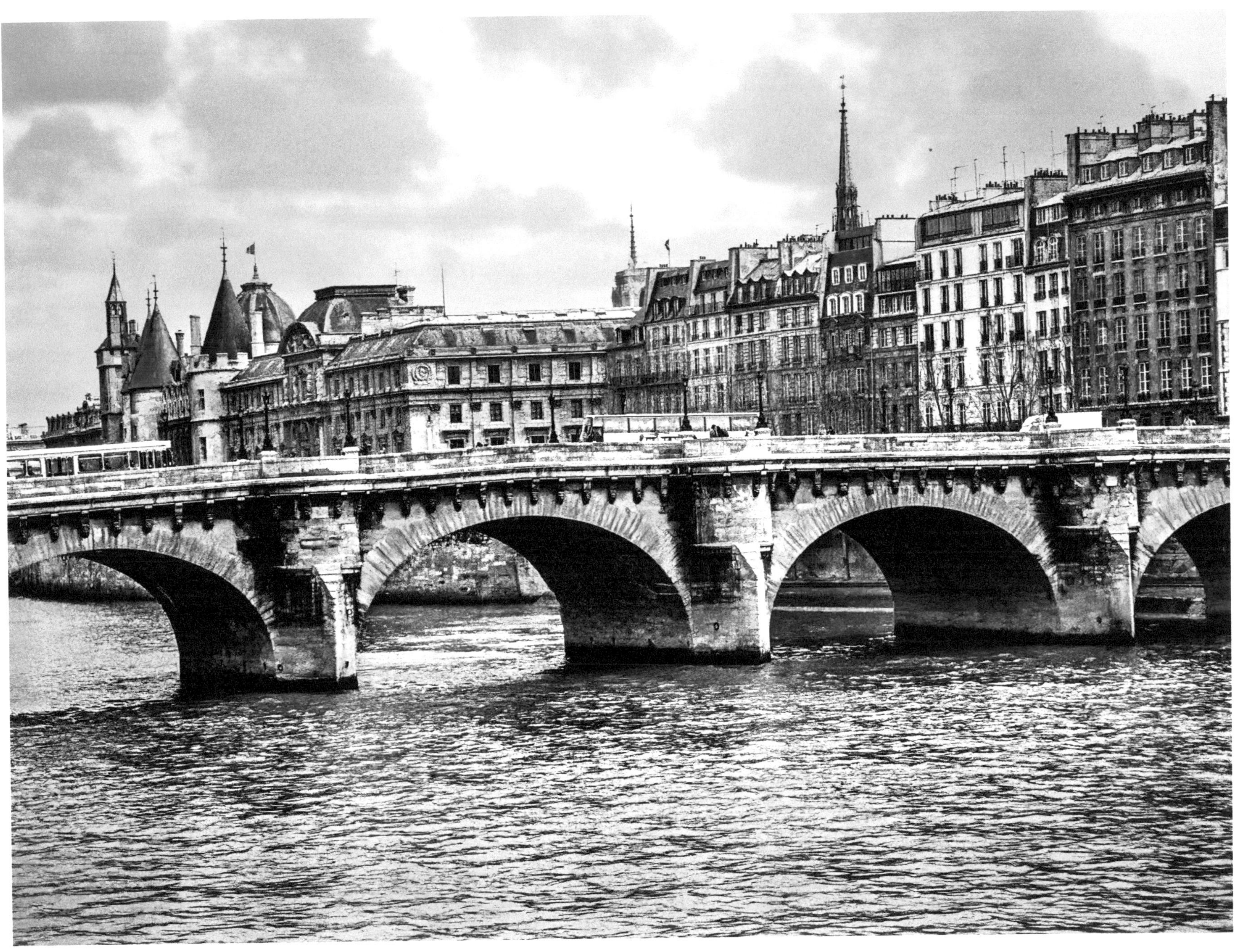

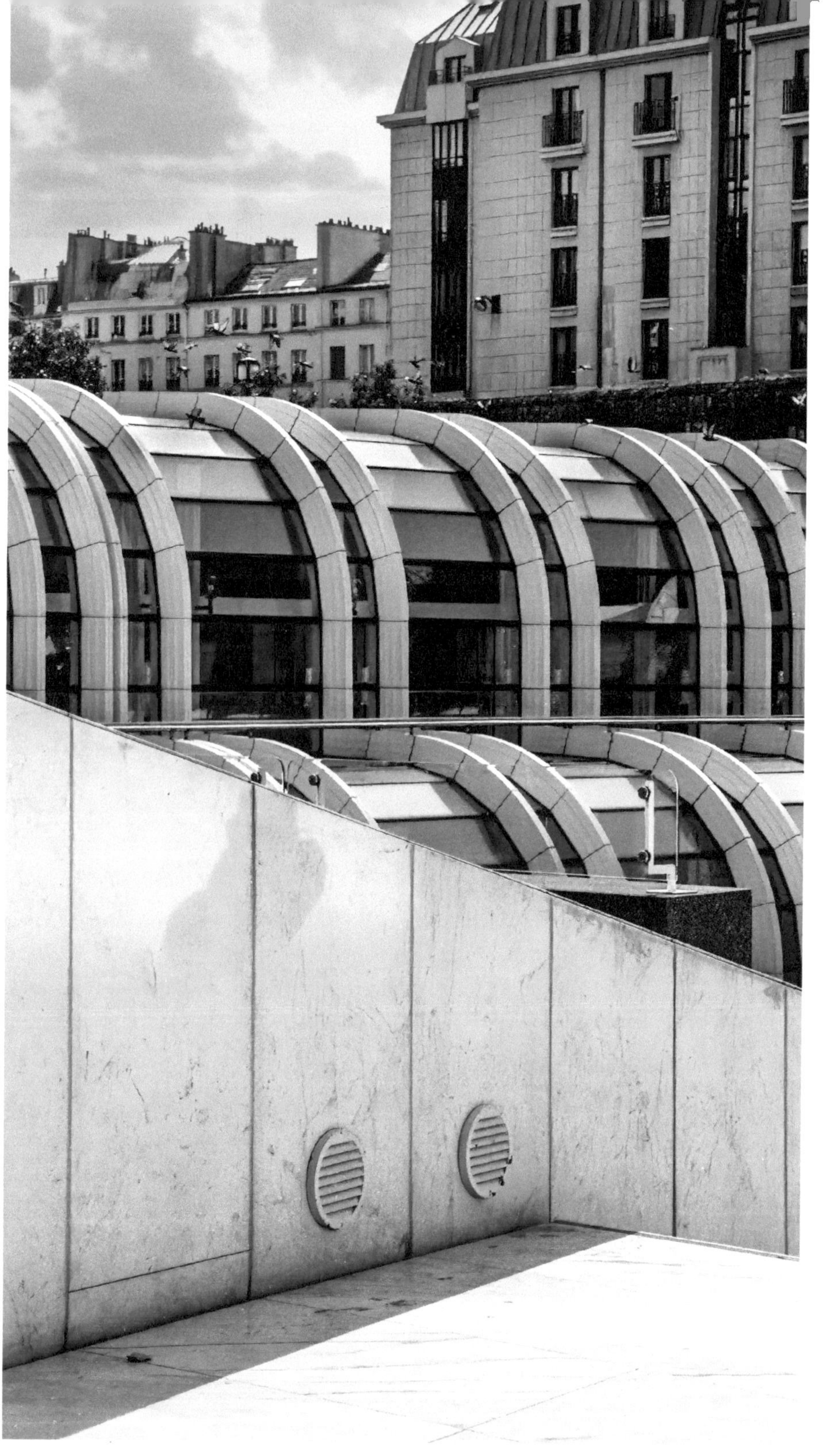

1st Arrondissement Les Halles or The Halls

This is a tiny window into the massive structure that is 'Les Halles.' It is home to Châtelet-Les Halles, a central train hub and one of the largest underground stations in the world. Opened in 1977, it is the central transit hub for the Paris metropolitan area, connecting three of five RER (Réseau Express Régional, or Regional Express Network) commuter-rail lines and five of sixteen Métro lines. The hub hosts 750,000 travelers per weekday (493,000 for the RER alone).

There is so much going on here that it is possible to stay underground and never see the light of day for as long as you wish. There are clothing and shoe stores, DIY shops, art galleries galore, and restaurants for every taste and budget.

Full orchestras often set up and play for the commuters coming and going, and street performers, both numerous and diverse, are everywhere, even on the trains. So there is always some form of entertainment happening.

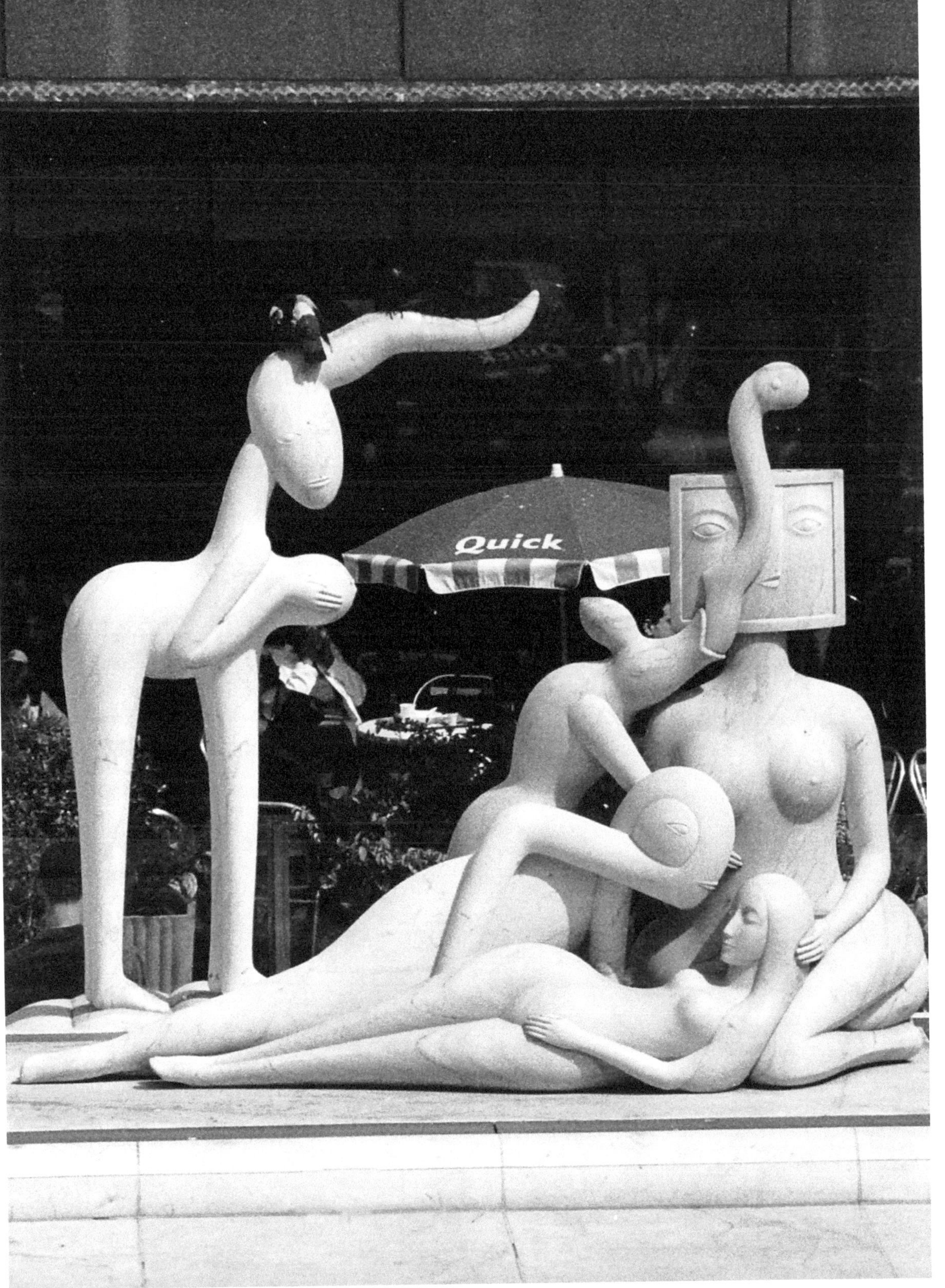

Pyegemalion, 1979,
Julio Silva (1930-2020),
in the Forum des Halles,
Paris, France

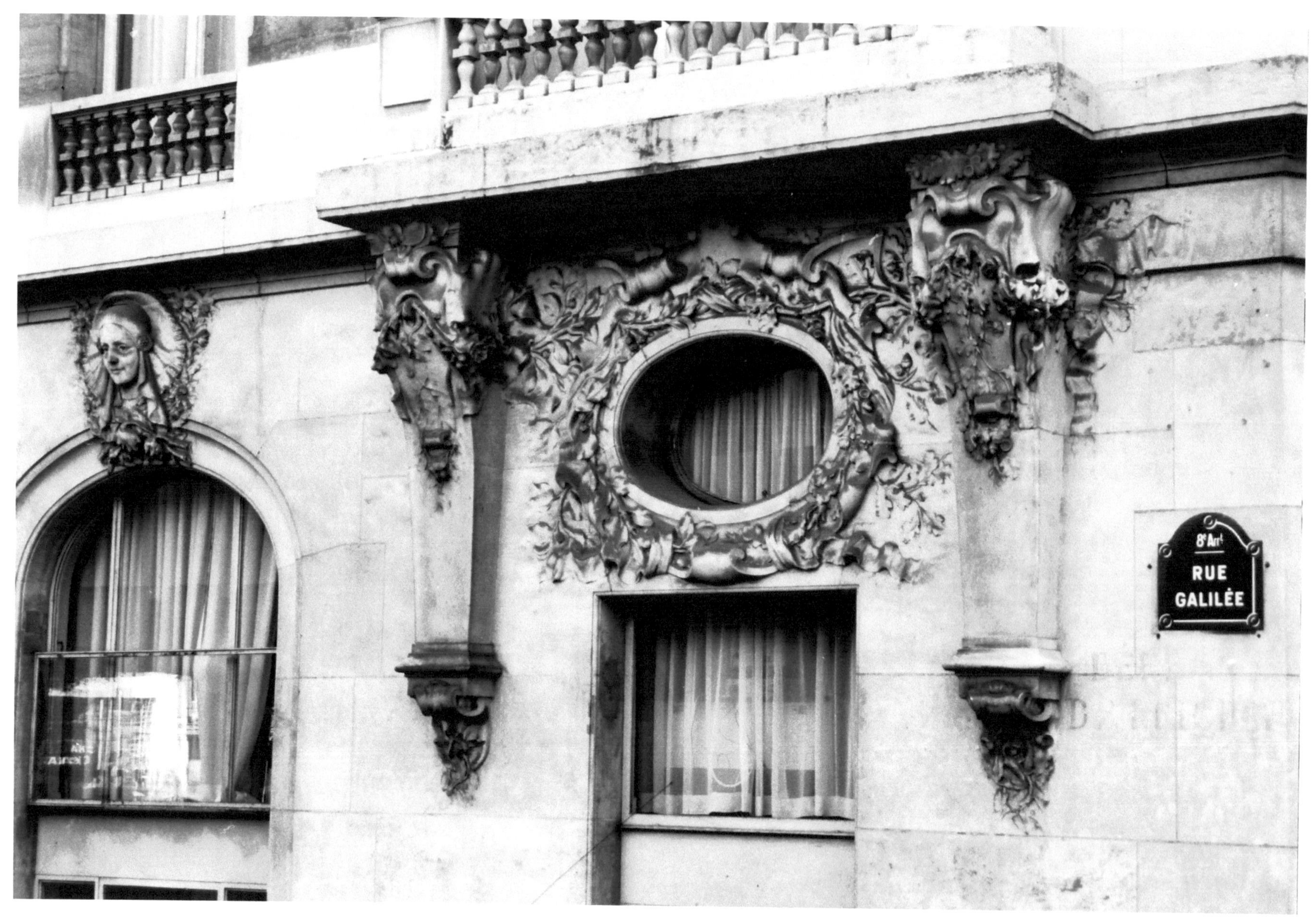

It's understandable to be in awe of the stunning architecture in Paris. The attention to detail and skilled craftsmanship required to create these buildings is truly impressive.

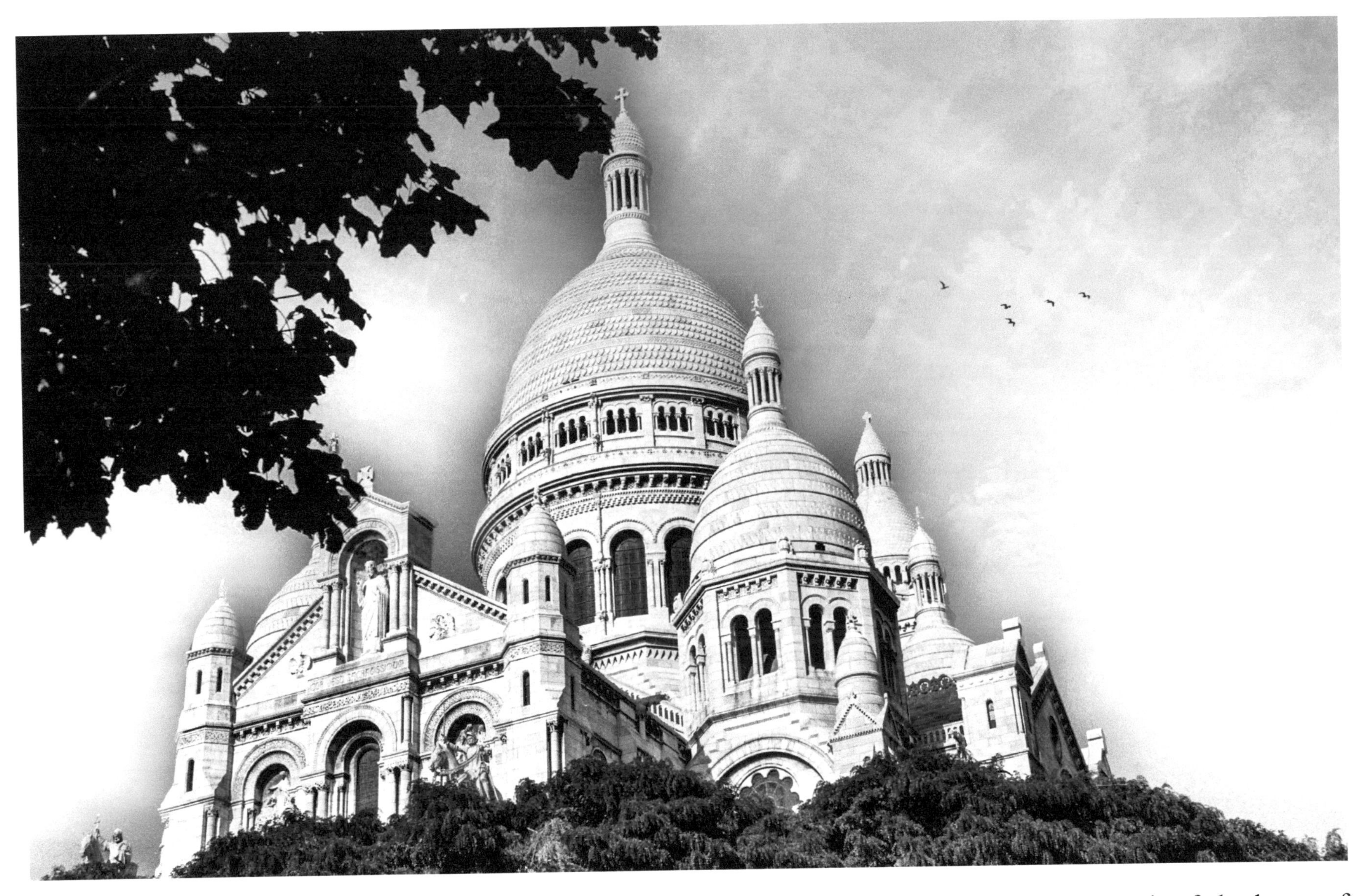

The **Sacré-Cœur Basilica** is a Roman Catholic church and minor basilica located at the summit of the butte of Montmartre in Paris, France. It is dedicated to the Sacred Heart of Jesus and was approved as a national historic monument in 2022. The basilica was proposed by Bishop Felix Fournier in 1870 and designed by Paul Abadie, with construction beginning in 1875 and lasting forty years.

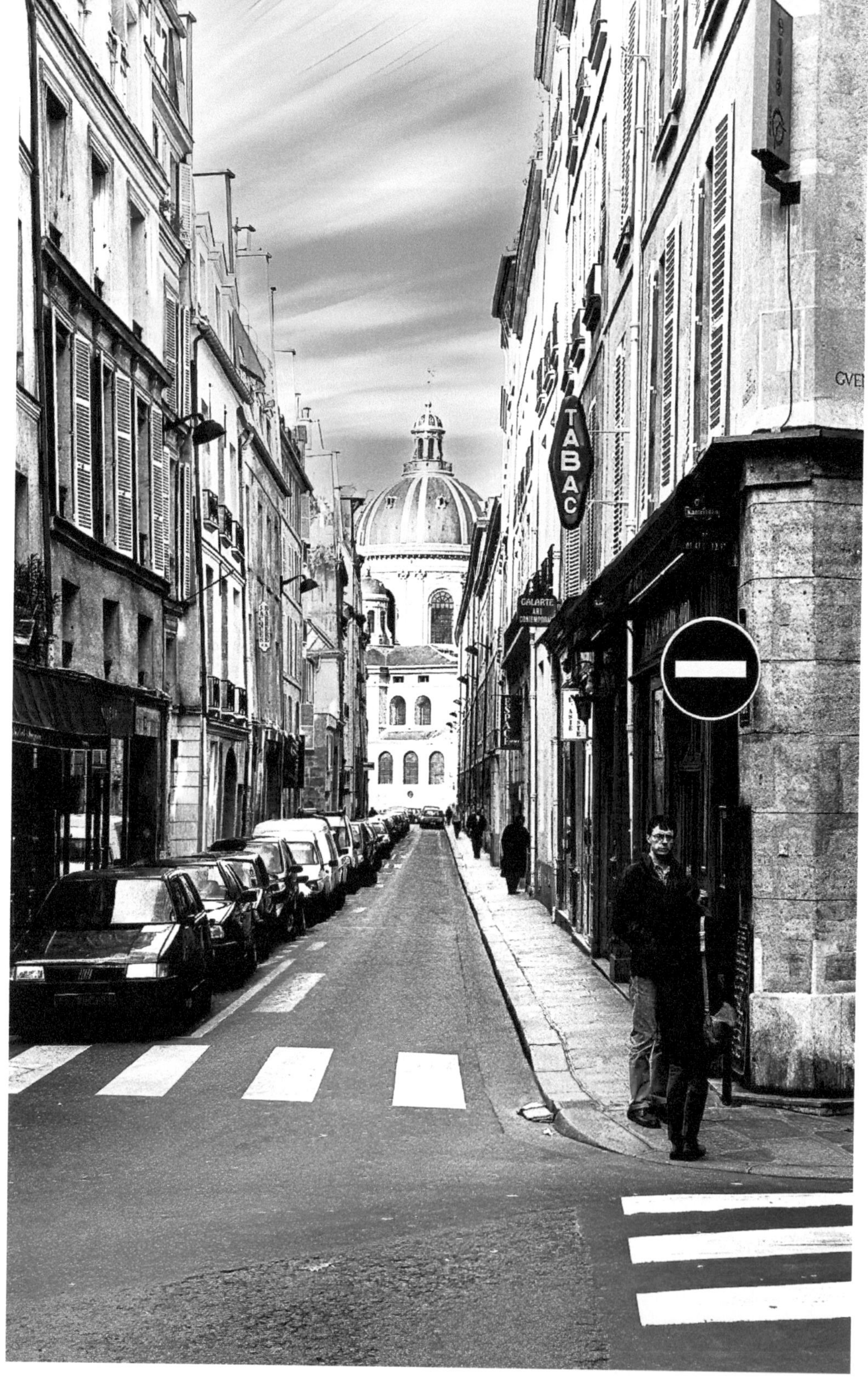

Rue Mazarine, seen from rue Guénégaud toward l'Institut de France, in the 6th arrondissement, 1868.

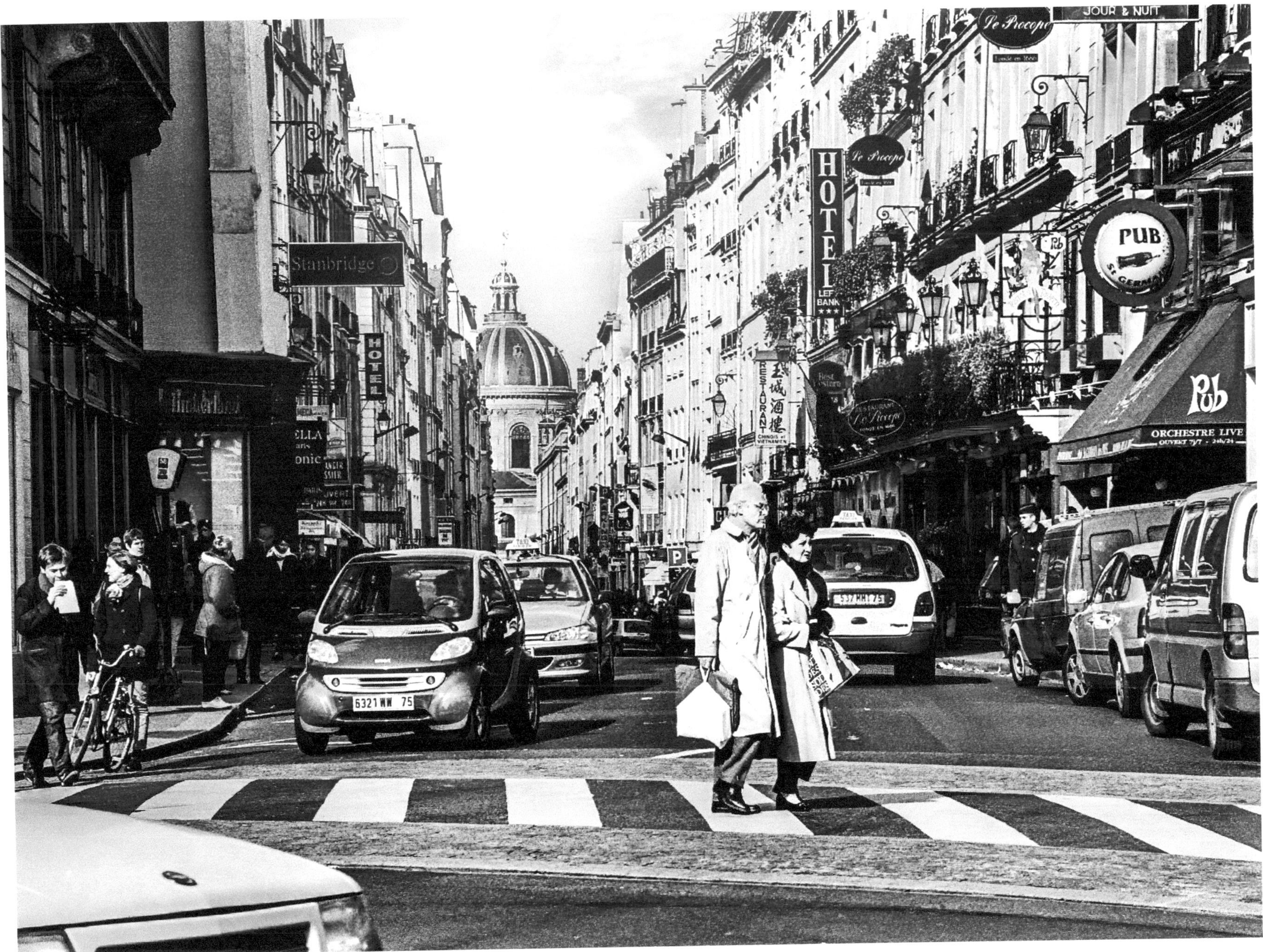

Le Procope
JOUR & NUIT
HOTEL
Stanbridge
PUB
ST GERMAIN
PUB
ORCHESTRE LIVE
HOTEL
RESTAURANT
6321 WW 75
TAXI

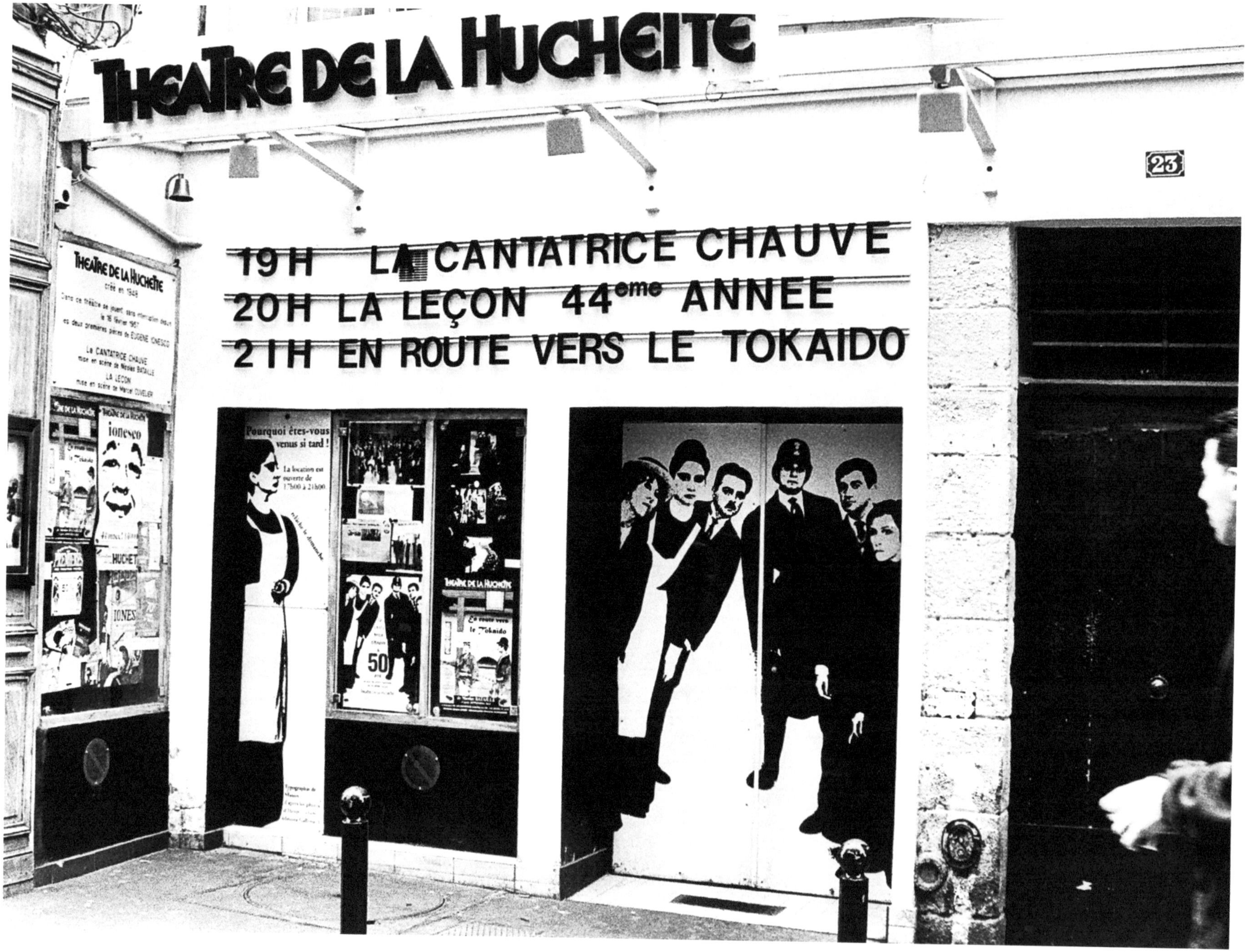

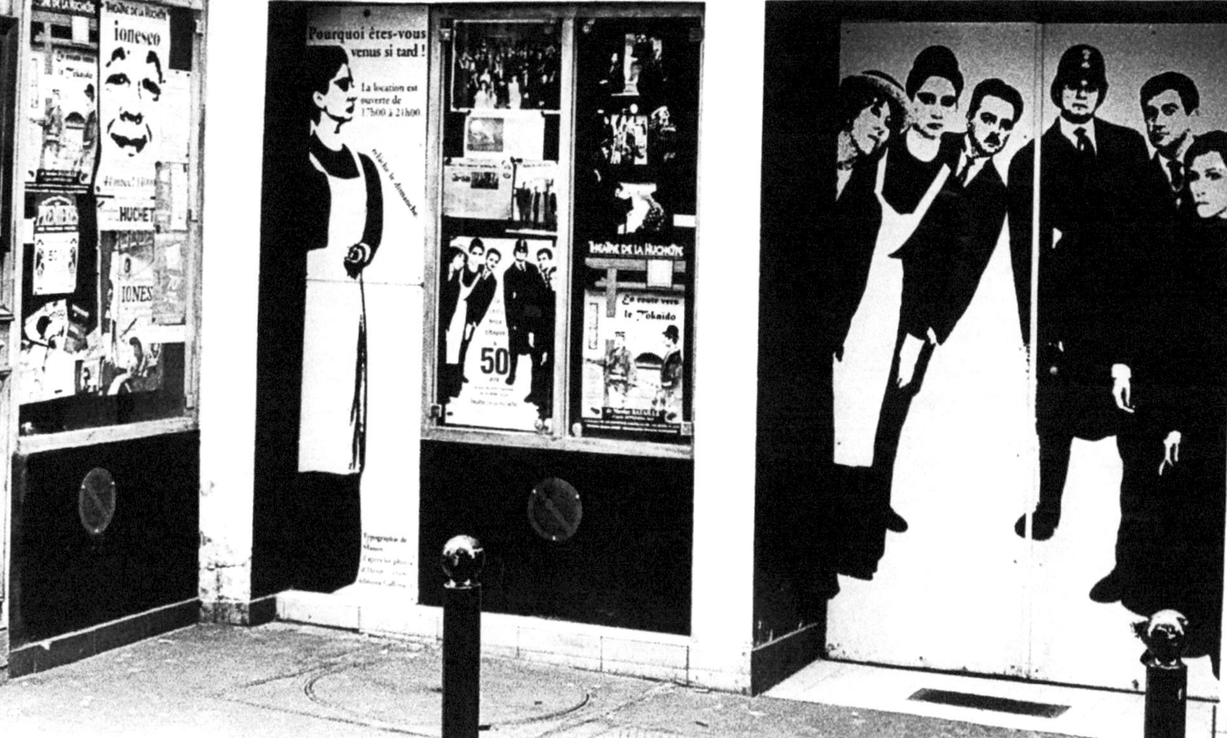

THEATRE DE LA HUCHETTE
23
19H   LA CANTATRICE CHAUVE
20H LA LEÇON 44ème ANNEE
21H EN ROUTE VERS LE TOKAIDO
THEATRE DE LA HUCHETTE
ionesco
Pourquoi êtes-vous venus si tard !
La location est ouverte de 17h00 à 21h00
THEATRE DE LA HUCHETTE
En route vers le Tokaido
50

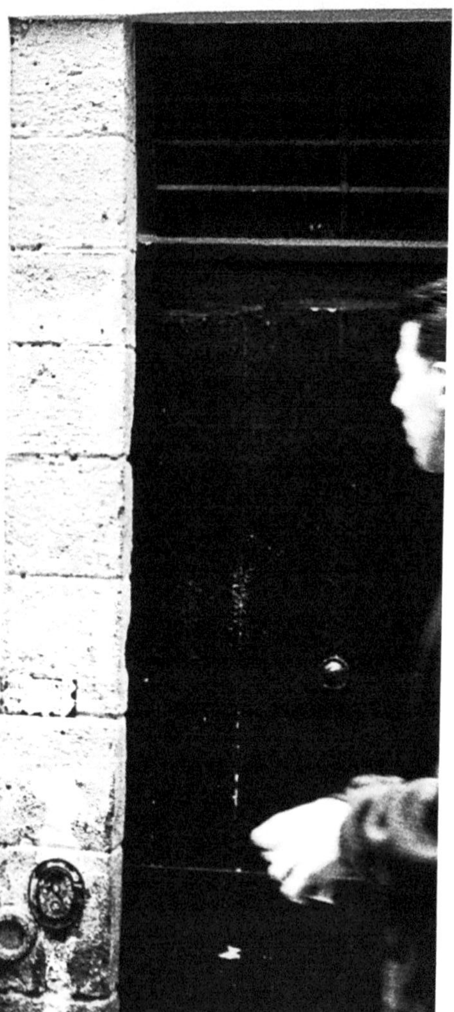

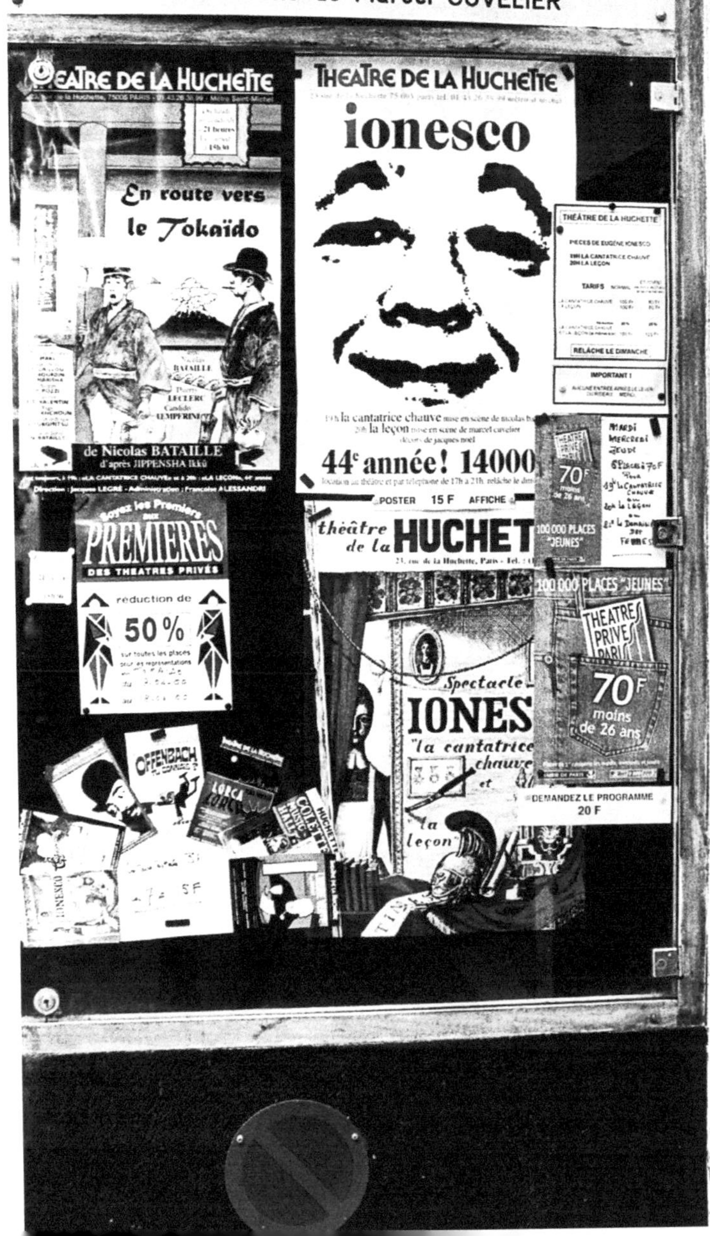

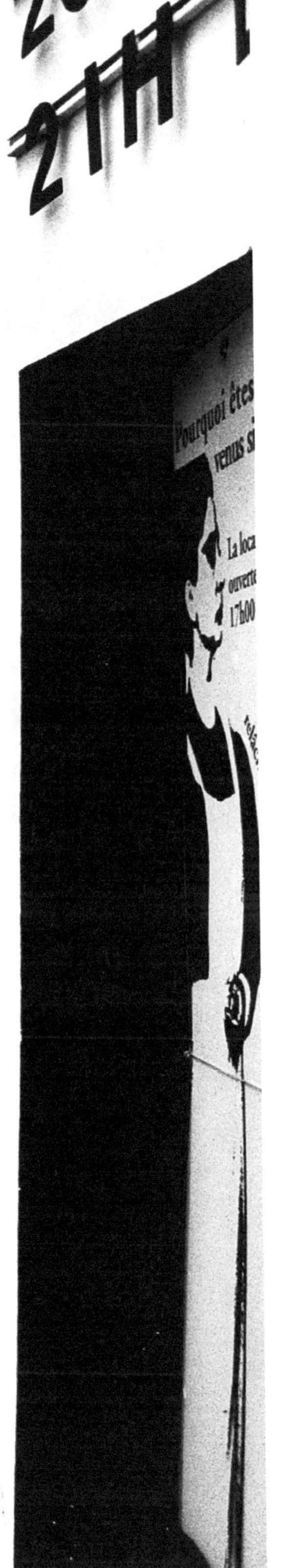

Théâtre de la Huchette
23, Rue de la Huchette, Paris 75005
Capacity 85 seats.
Duration 1 hour, No intermission.

Details:
Classic French play for all audiences in French with English subtitles on specific dates.

Highlights:
The Lesson (La Leçon): A seemingly innocent exchange in which a shy, older teacher meets an outspoken student.

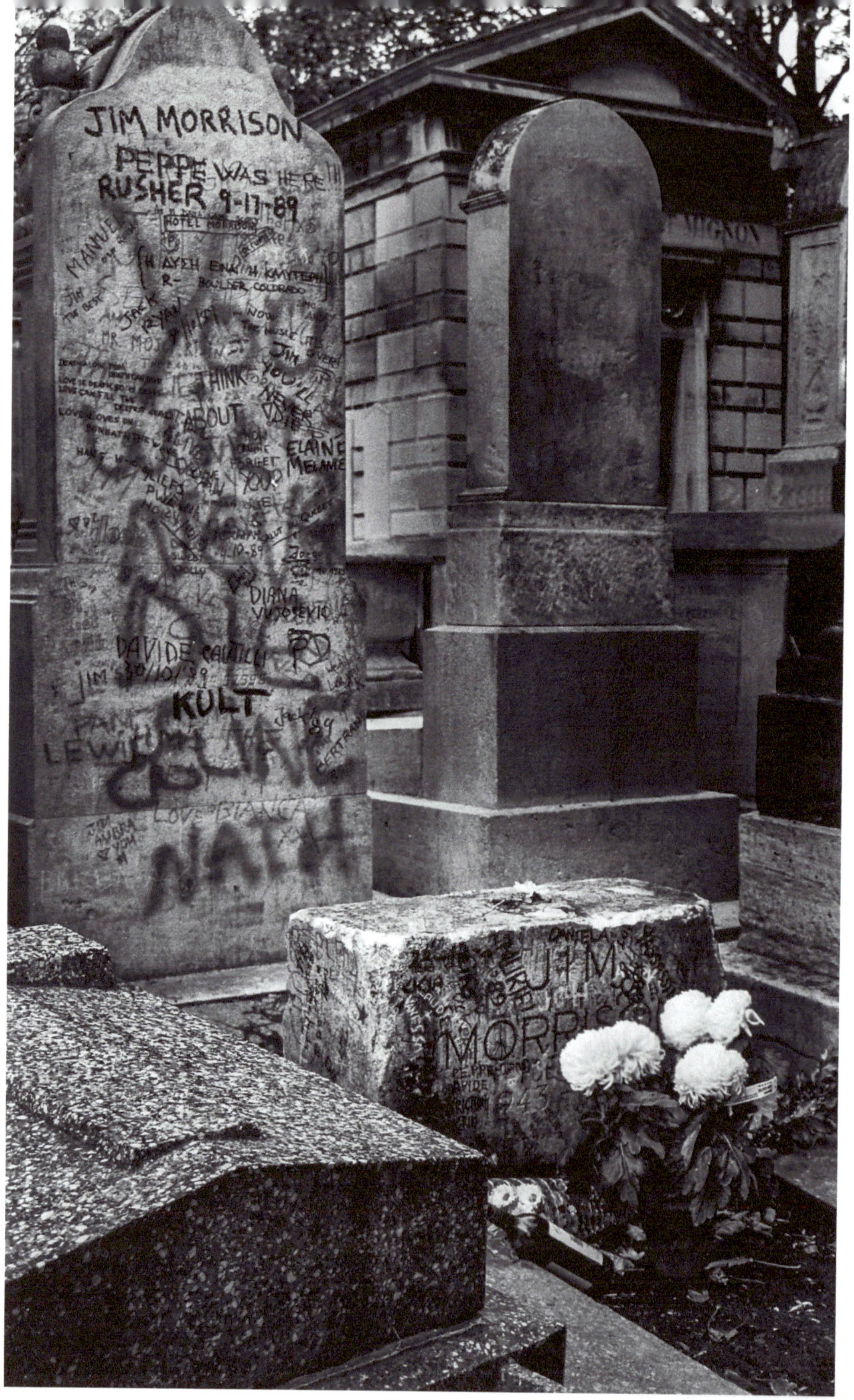

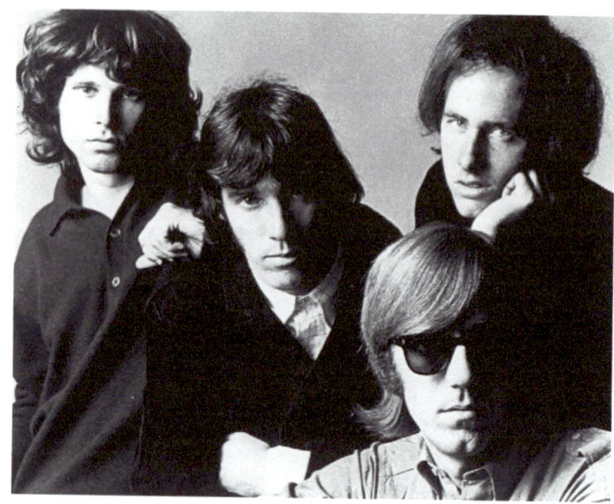

Michael Ochs Archives/Getty Images

The Doors: (from left) Jim Morrison, John Densmore, Ray Manzarek (foreground), and Robby Krieger

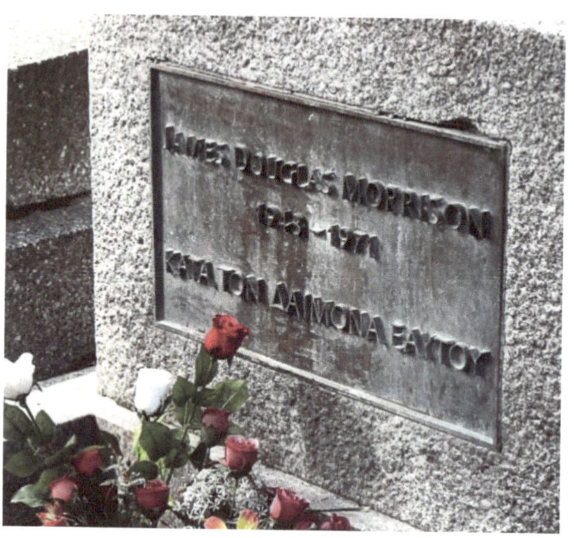

© BMCL/Shutterstock.com

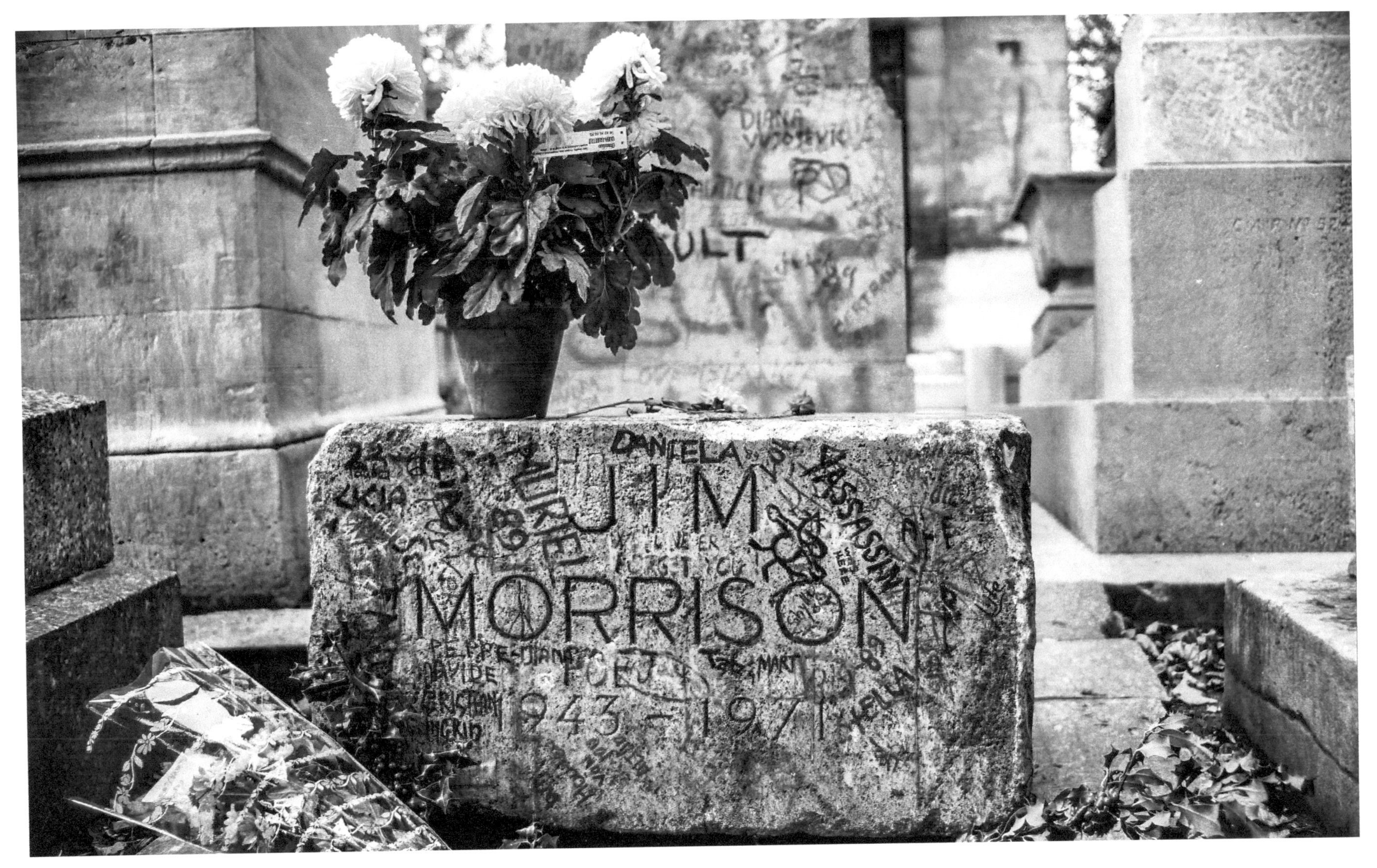

Jim Morrison's grave site used to be a popular spot for parties but is now guarded by two closed-circuit TVs due to the large crowds that can gather there, reaching over 300 people during peak hours. Fans come from all over the world, and even shops outside the cemetery cater to the Doors mania by selling T-shirts with Morrison's portrait on them. There is a new headstone and gate to keep visitors at a safe distance.

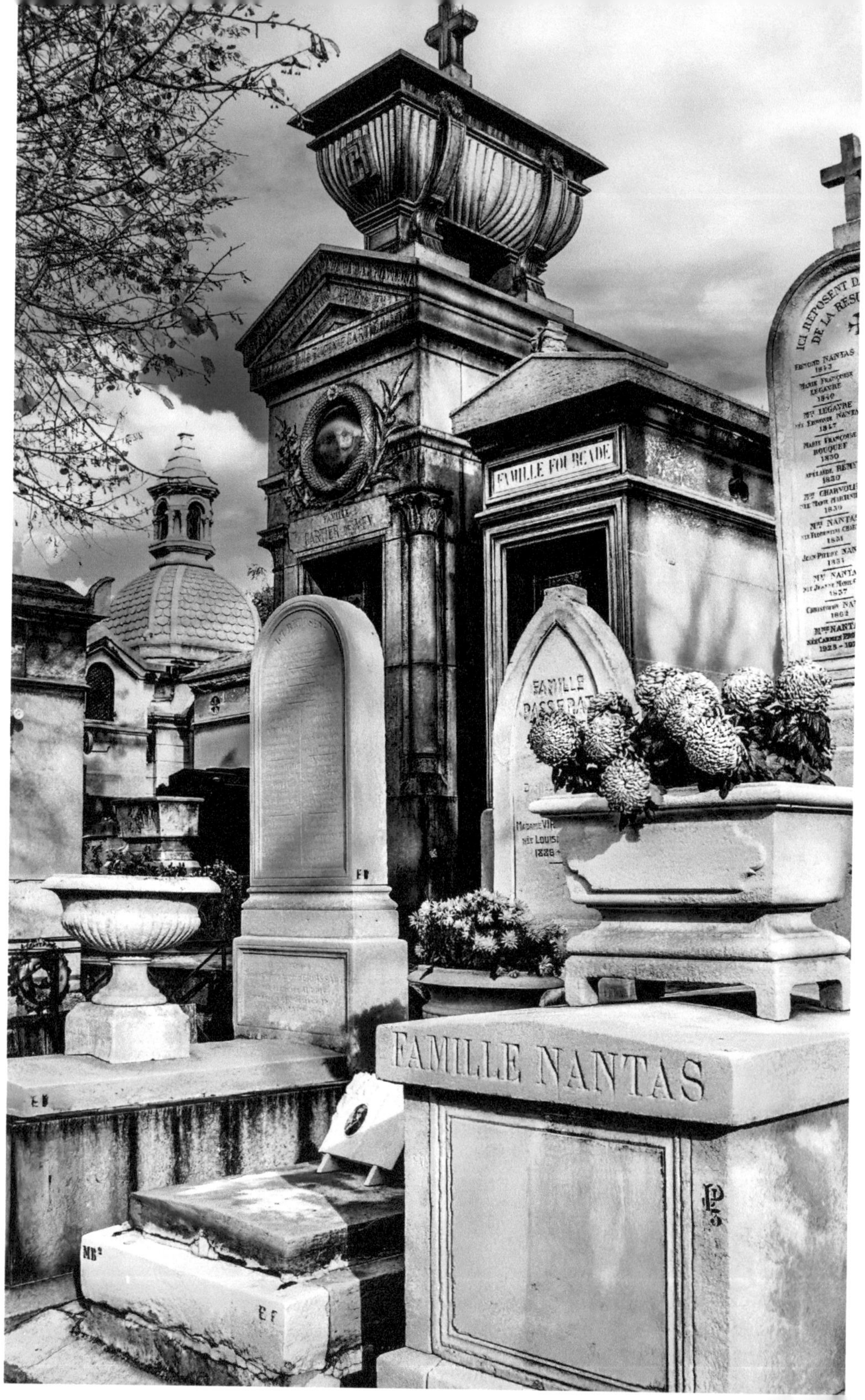

Père Lachaise Cemetery

16, Rue du Repos 75020 Paris is both the largest park and nondenominational cemetery on the northeast side of Paris.

With nearly 3 million visitors a year, it is a beautiful way to spend an afternoon strolling through the tombstones of some of the most influential creatives, royals, politicians, and philosophers.

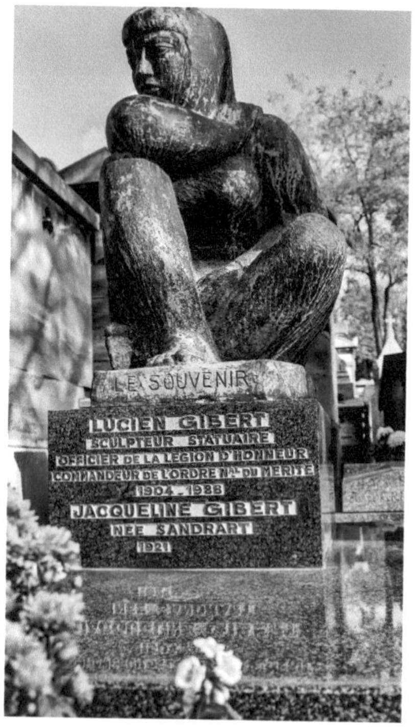

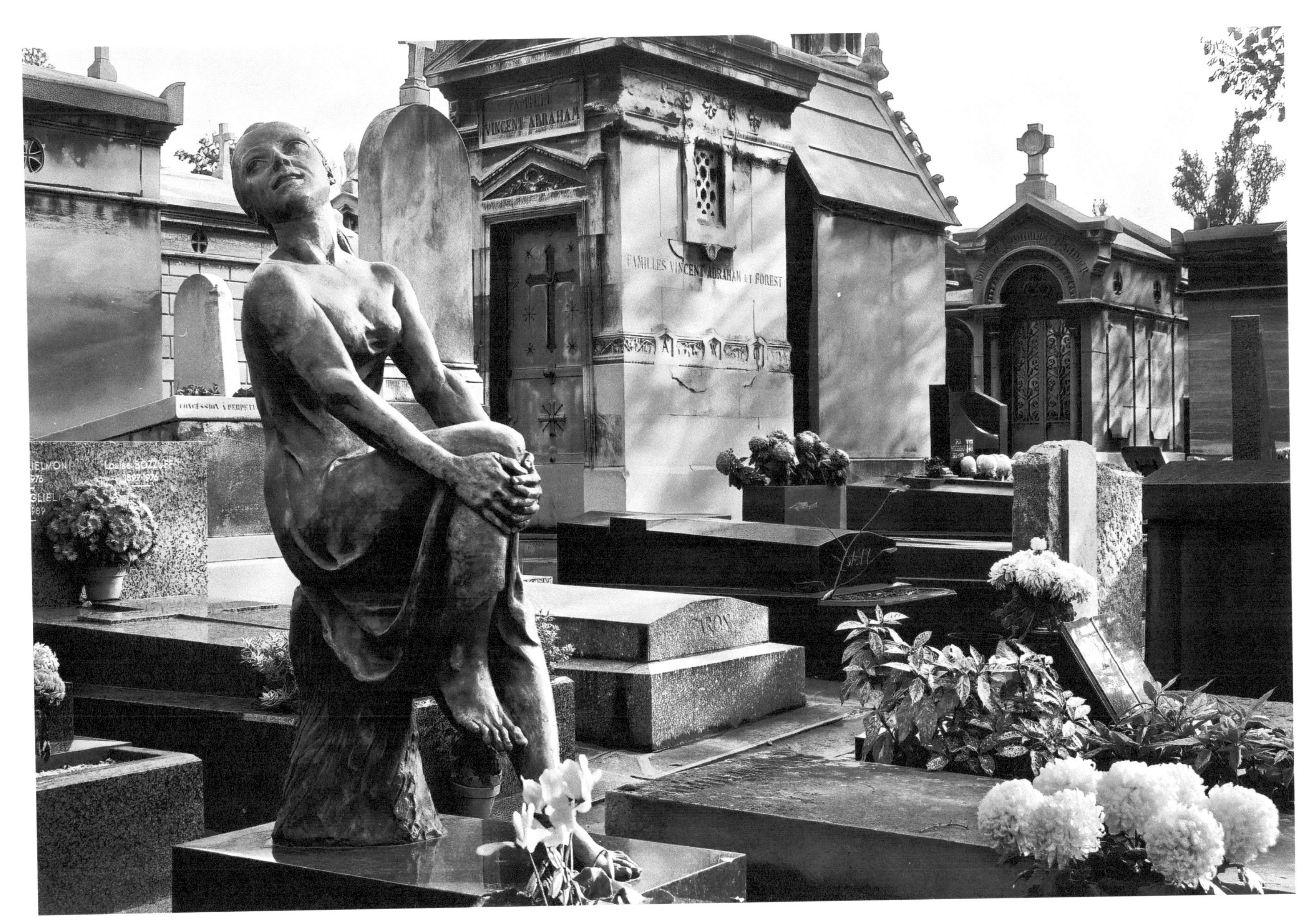

Remina Maggiori (1912-1985)
Bronze statue created in Florence by Italian sculptor and painter Marcello Tommasi (1928-2008)

"History is not a burden on the memory but an illumination of the soul."

-Lord Acton (1834-1902), English Catholic historian, politician, and writer

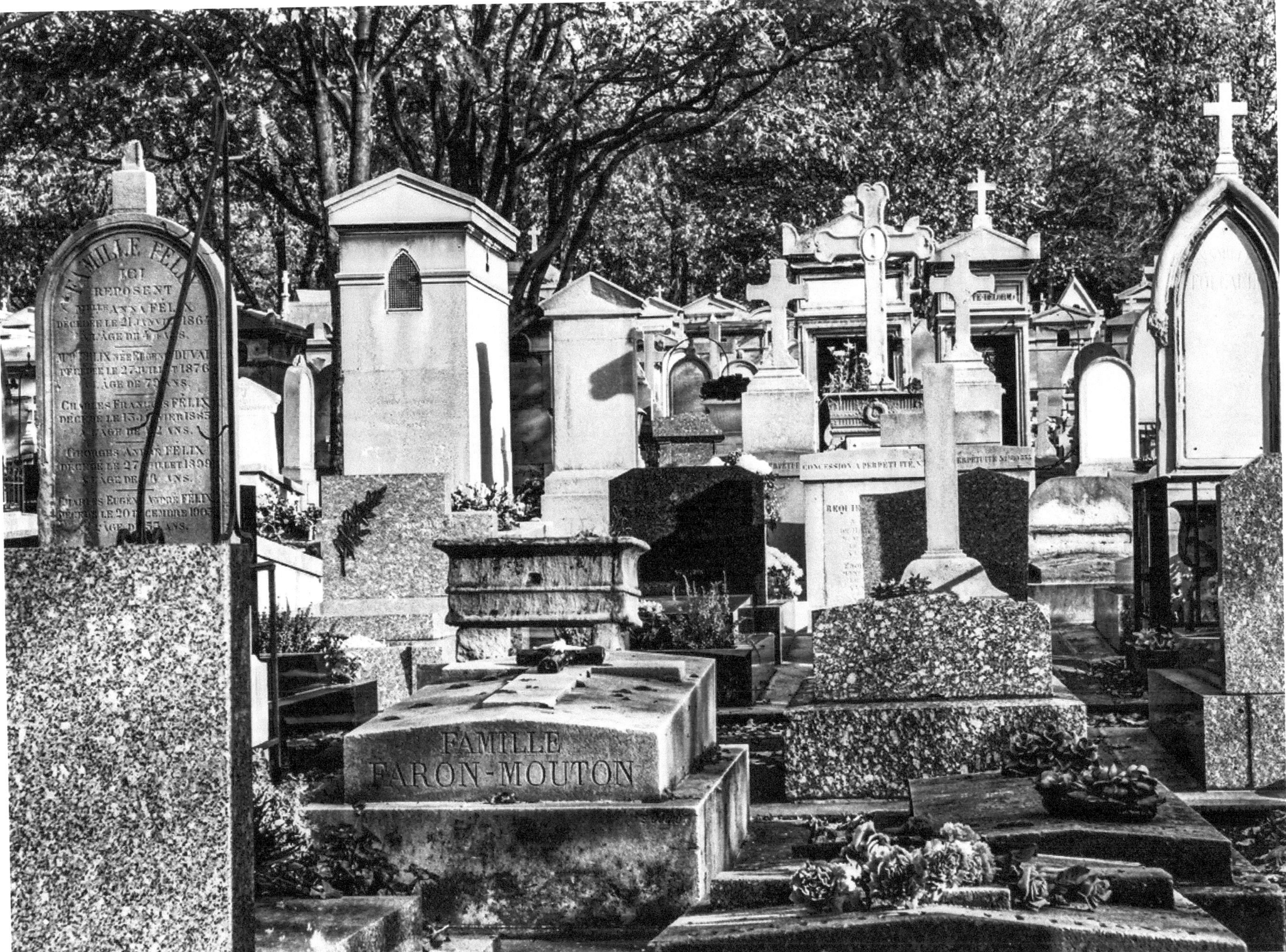

FAMILLE
FARON-MOUTON

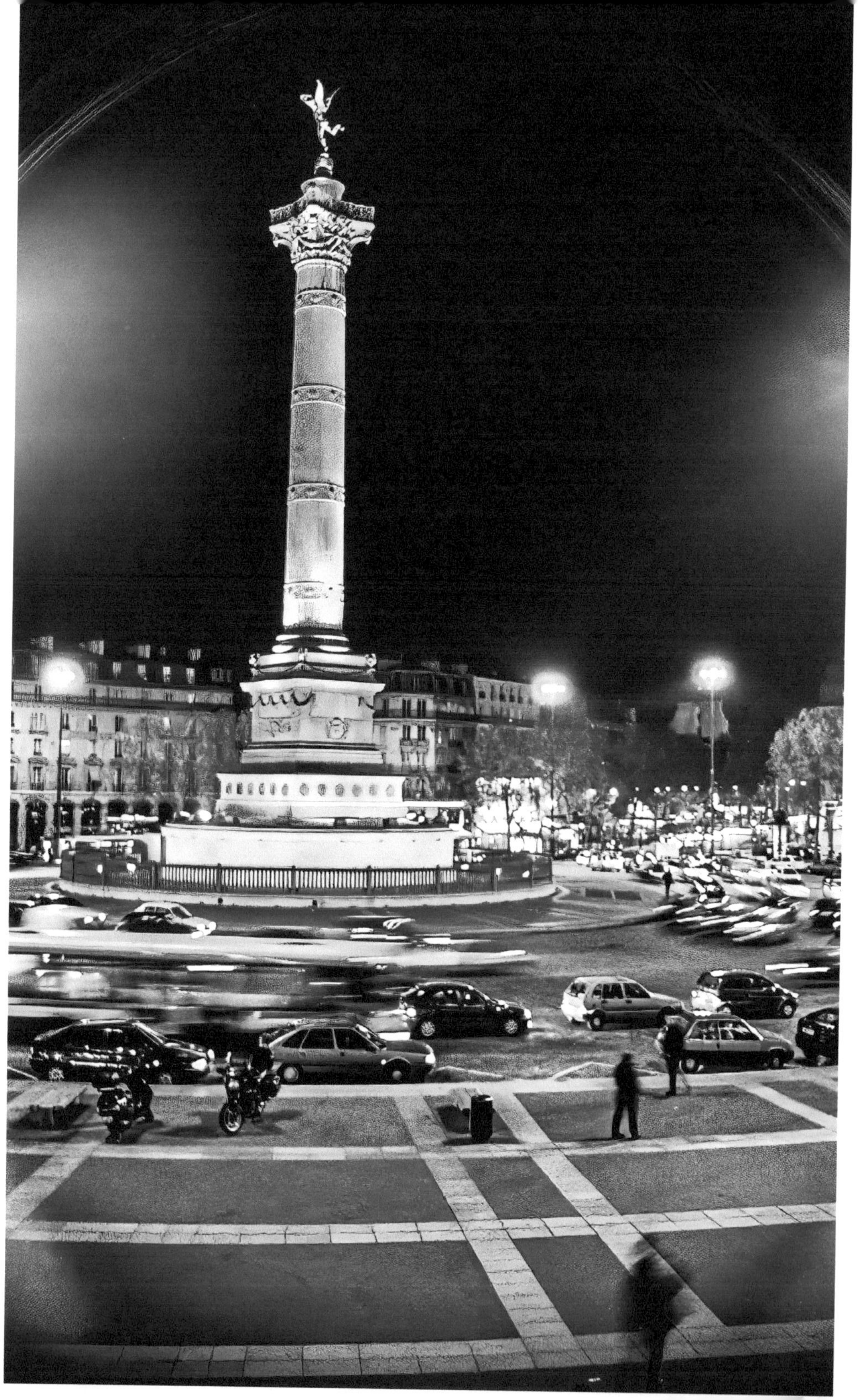

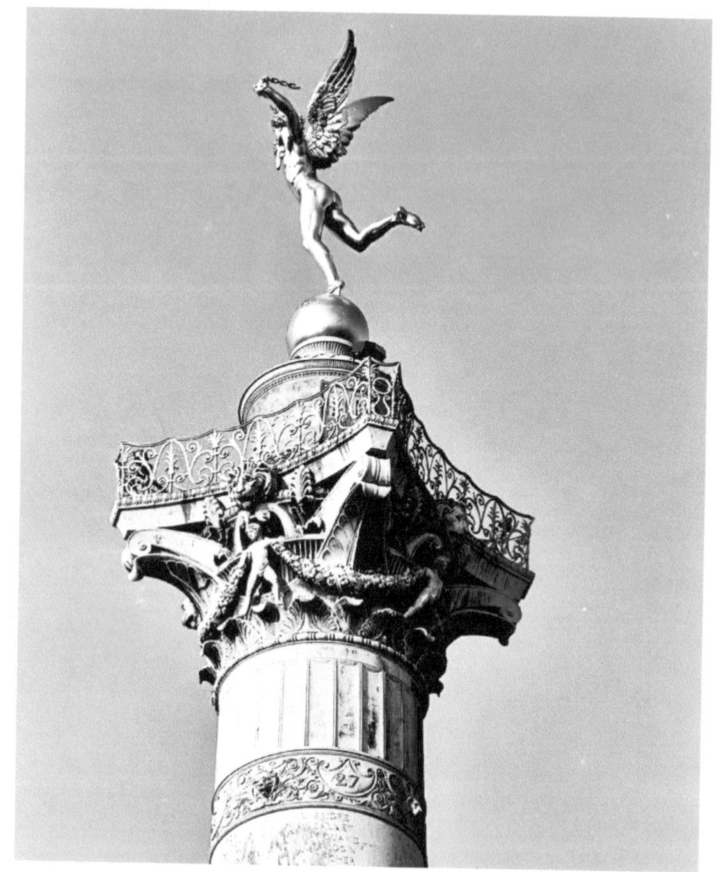

The July Column is a prominent monument in Paris commemorating the Revolution of 1830. It stands in the center of the Place de la Bastille. It celebrates the "Trois Glorieuses," the *three glorious* days of 27–29 July 1830 that saw the fall of Charles X, King of France, and the commencement of the "July Monarchy" of Louis-Philippe, King of the French.

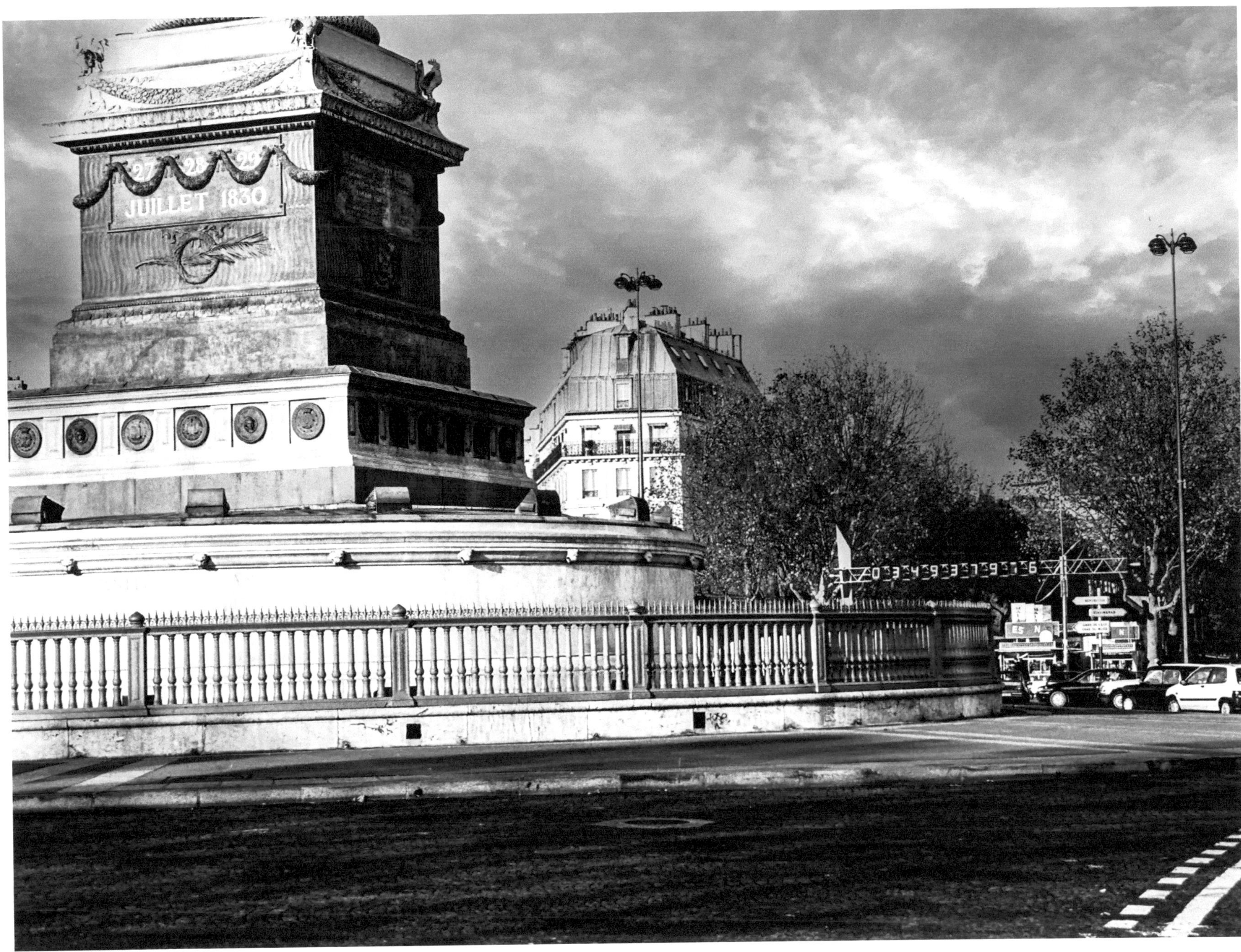

27 28 29
JUILLET 1830

"When you feel you have achieved perfect symmetry in any given image, you excitedly press the shutter button, and voilà, you have captured a timeless image."
-Chuck Waite (1955), Happily retired family man

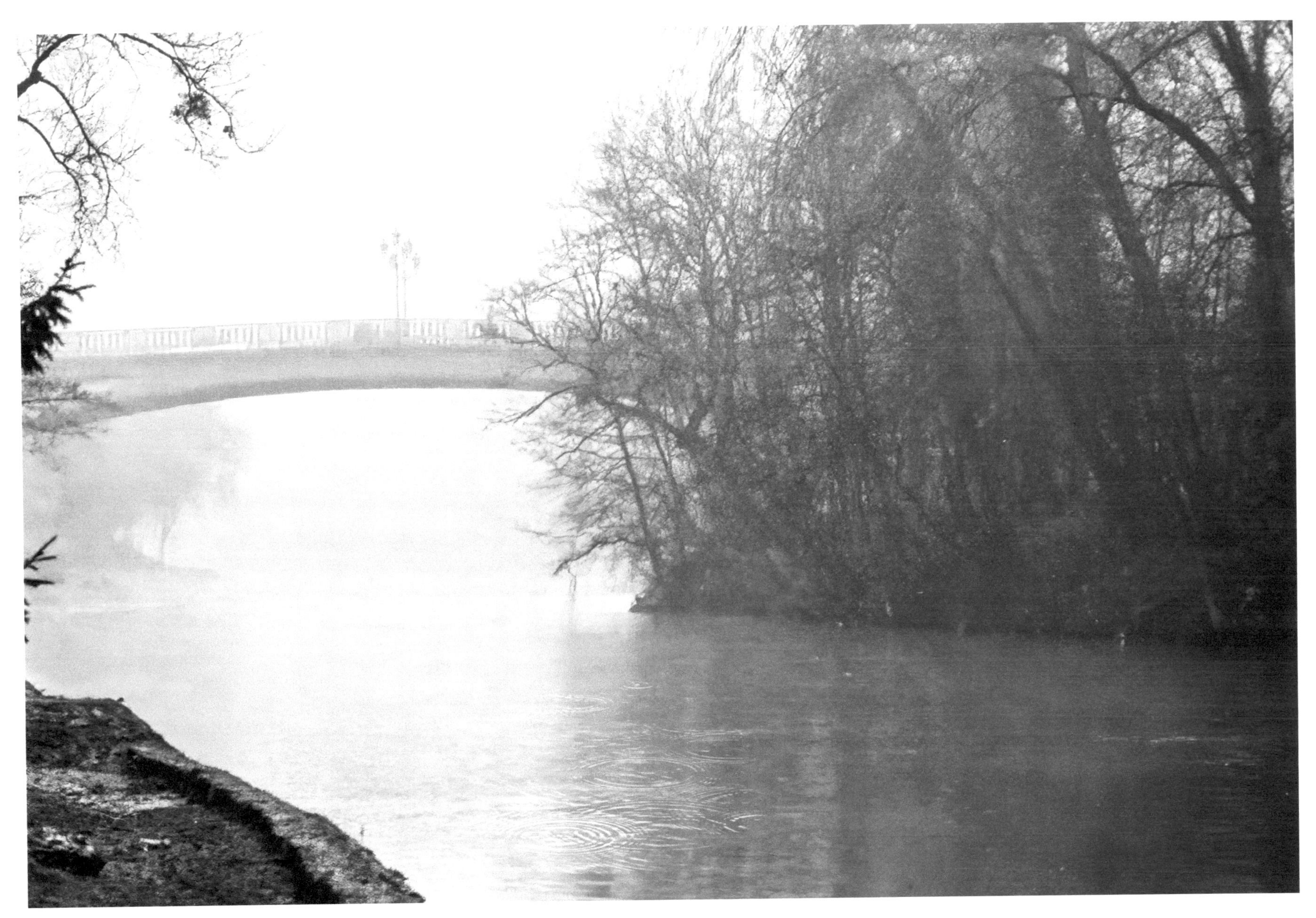

Saint-Maur-des-Fossés, La Varenne-Saint-Hilaire

La Marne -The Marne River at 326 miles/525 km, East of the Paris Basin, is the longest river in France.

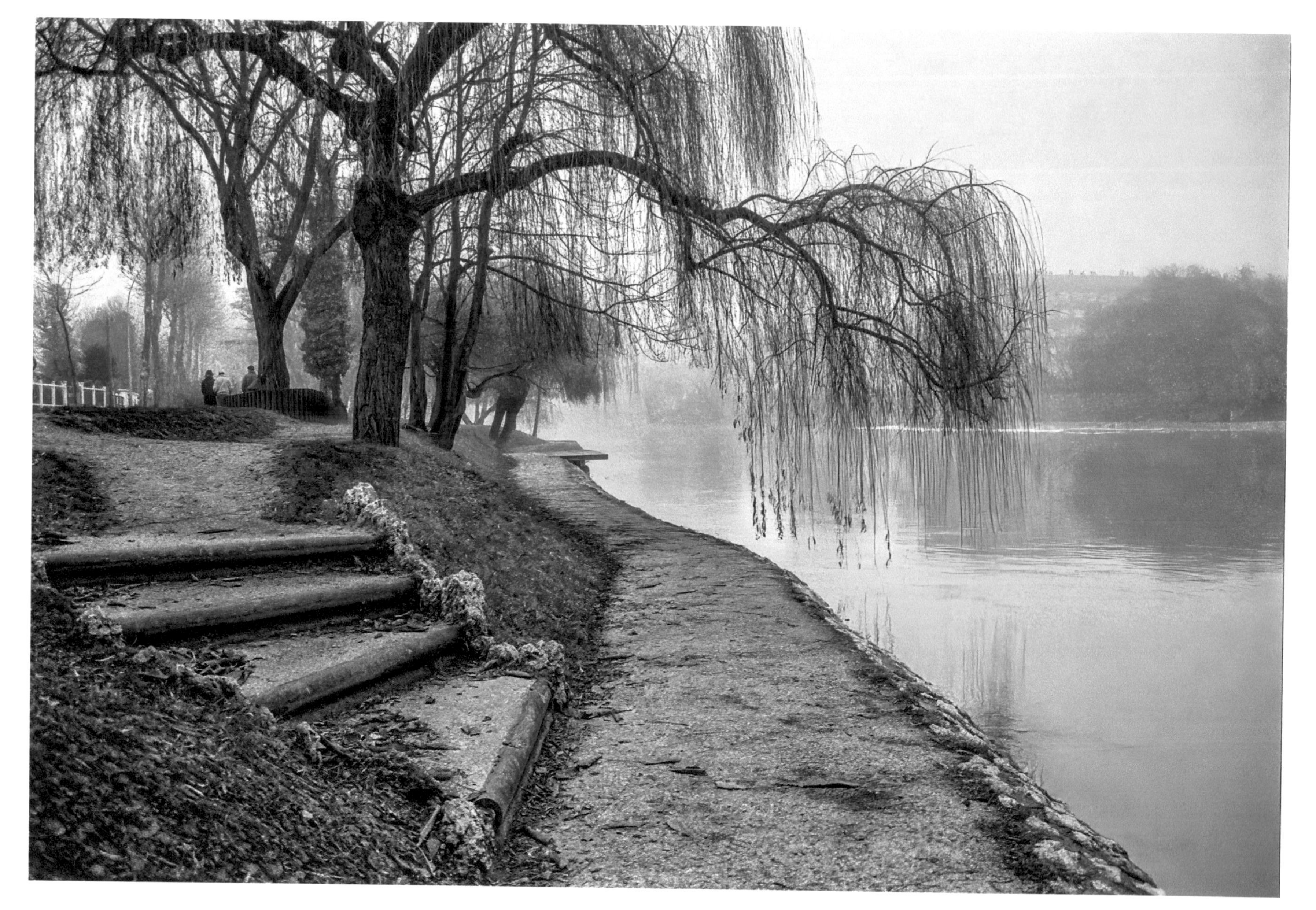

Walking along the river was like taking your soul out for a good cleaning, no matter the time of day, the season, or the weather.

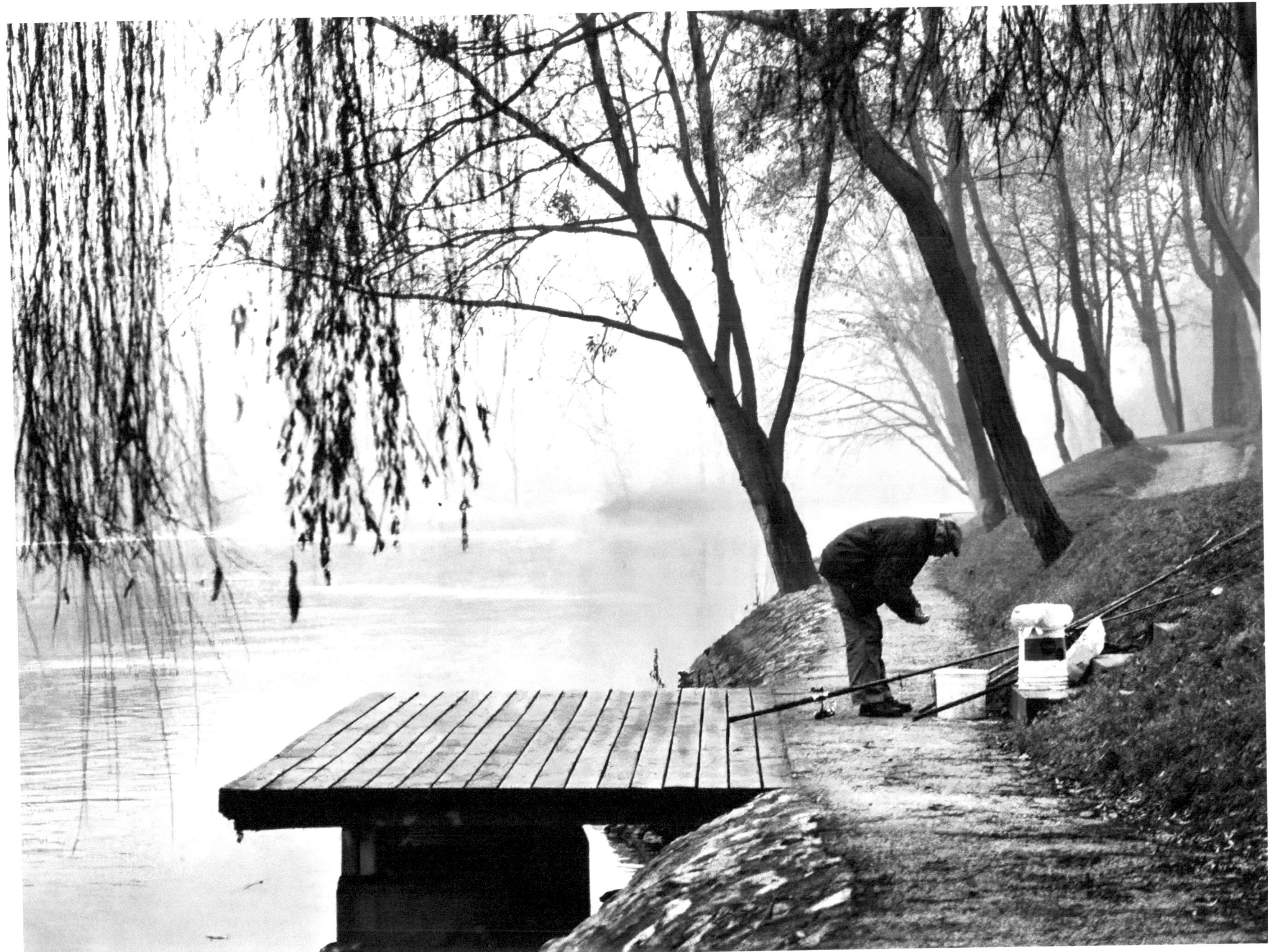

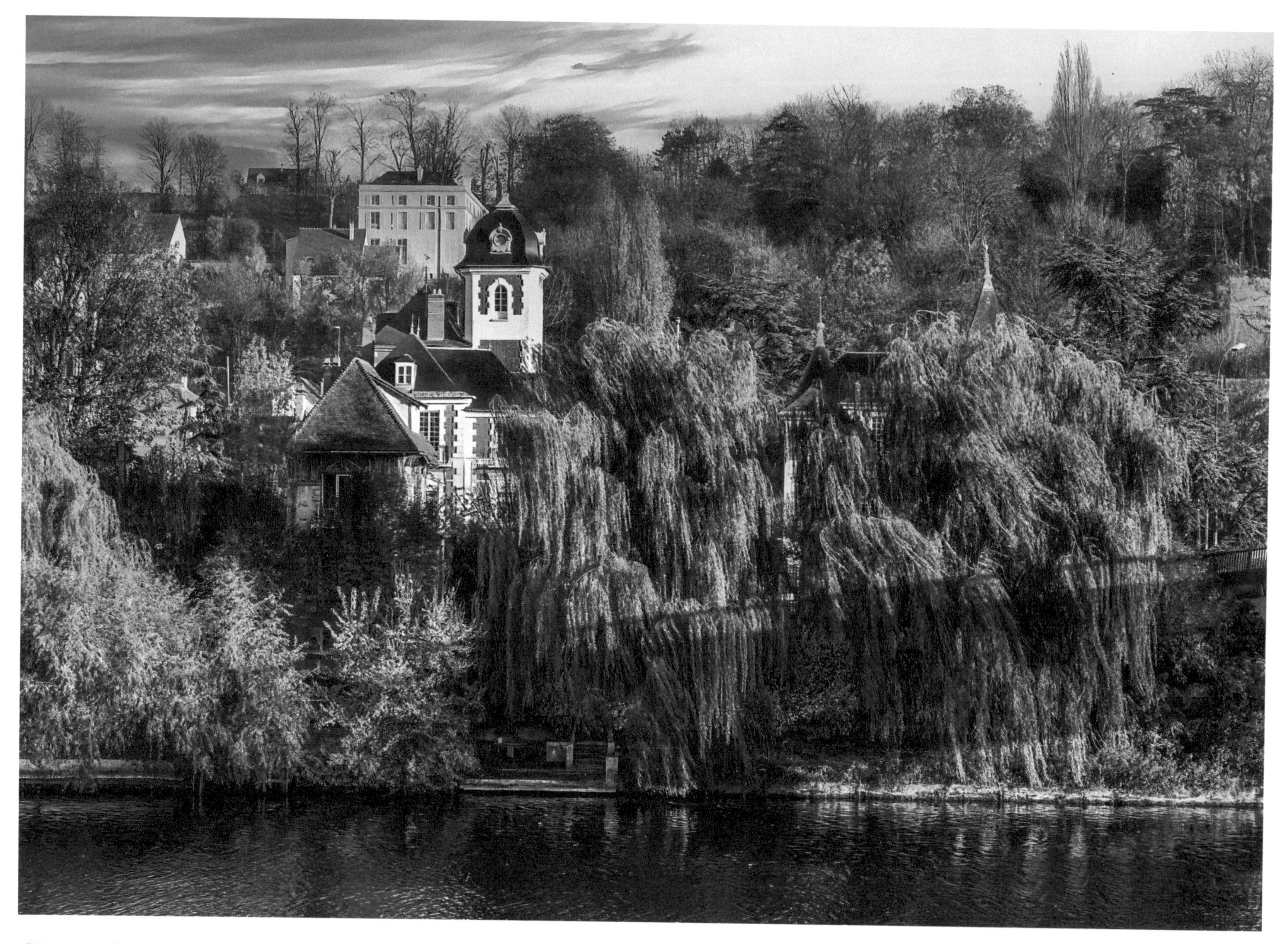

Chenneviéres-sur-Marne across the river from La Varenne-Saint-Hilaire

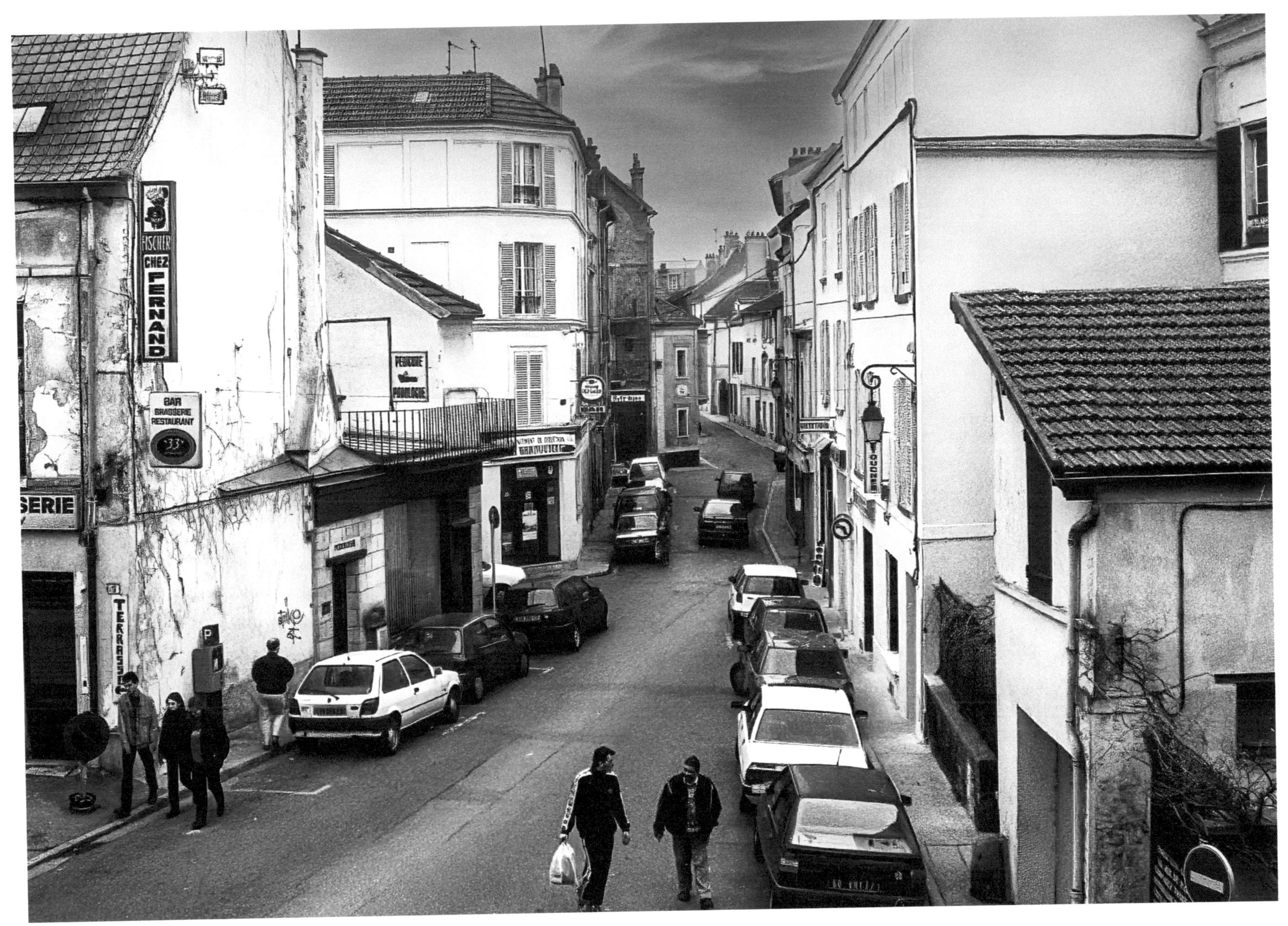

Lagny-sur-Marne, France

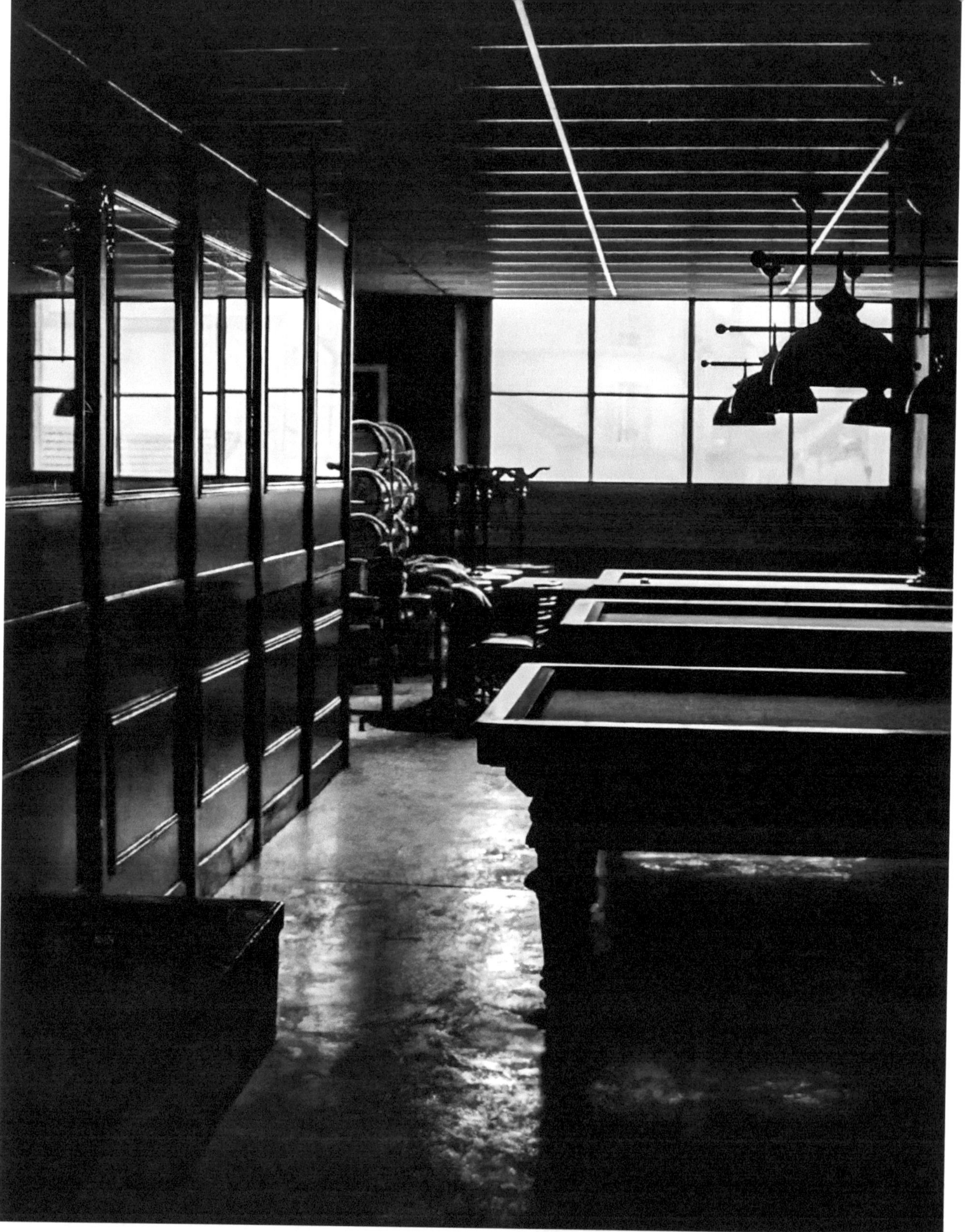

Even in the silence I could still hear the voices from the past.

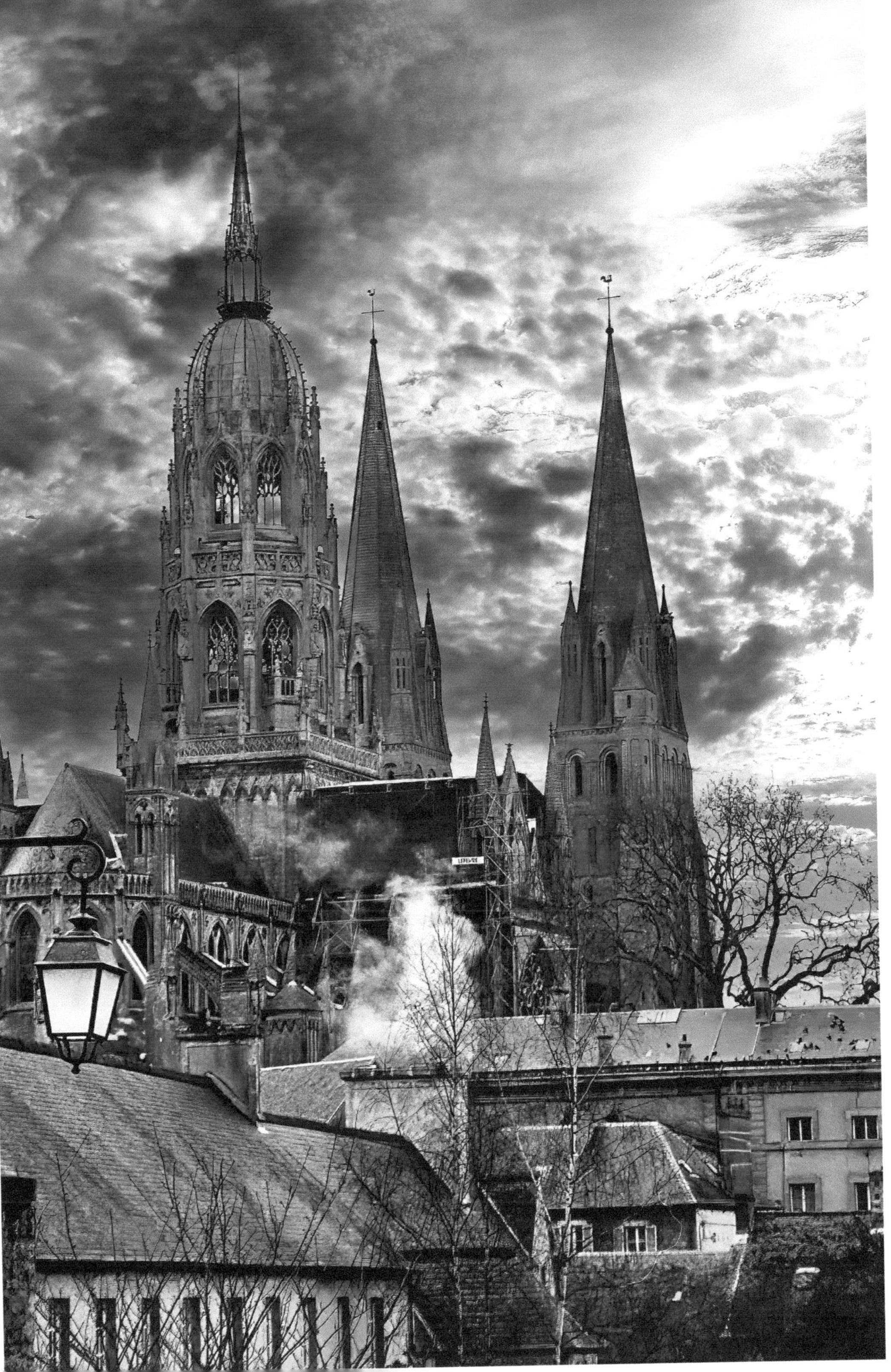

Normandy

A region known for its rich history, Normandy has diverse landscapes and strong connections to legendary figures like William the Conquerer and Joan of Arc. It features picturesque pastures, ancient fishing harbors, sun-drenched seaside resorts, towering gothic cathedrals, and apple orchards that produce the region's famed cider. The Bayeux Tapestry, a thousand-year-old tapestry that tells the story of medieval warfare and sieges, can be found in Normandy. The region is also the birthplace of Impressionism, with the artists finding a common muse in Normandy's landscapes.

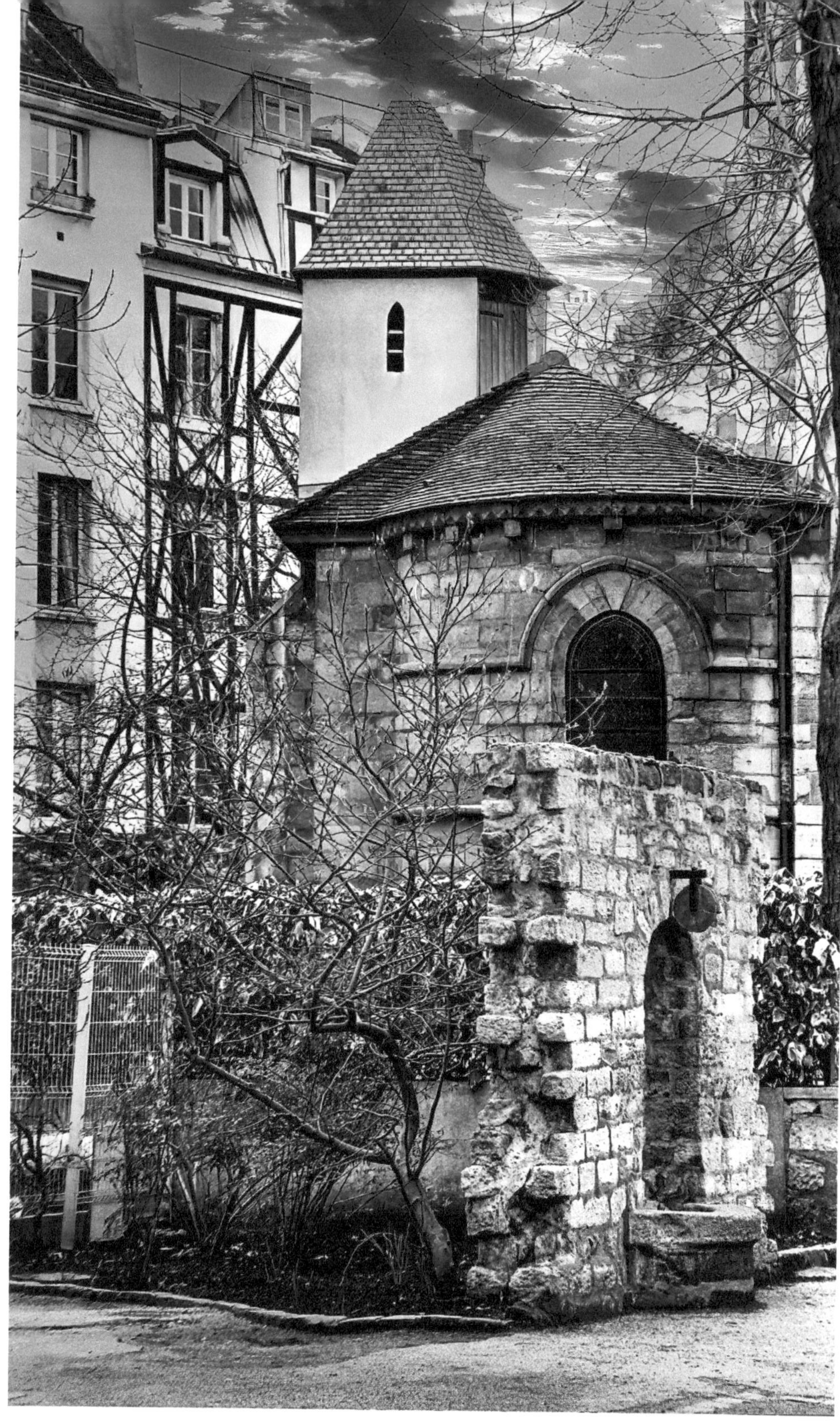

"Images captured in a photograph are as unique and individual as a snowflake. Emotions stirred and reactions to any given image are very personal, and no two people will perceive an image the same."
-Chuck Waite (1955), Happily retired family man

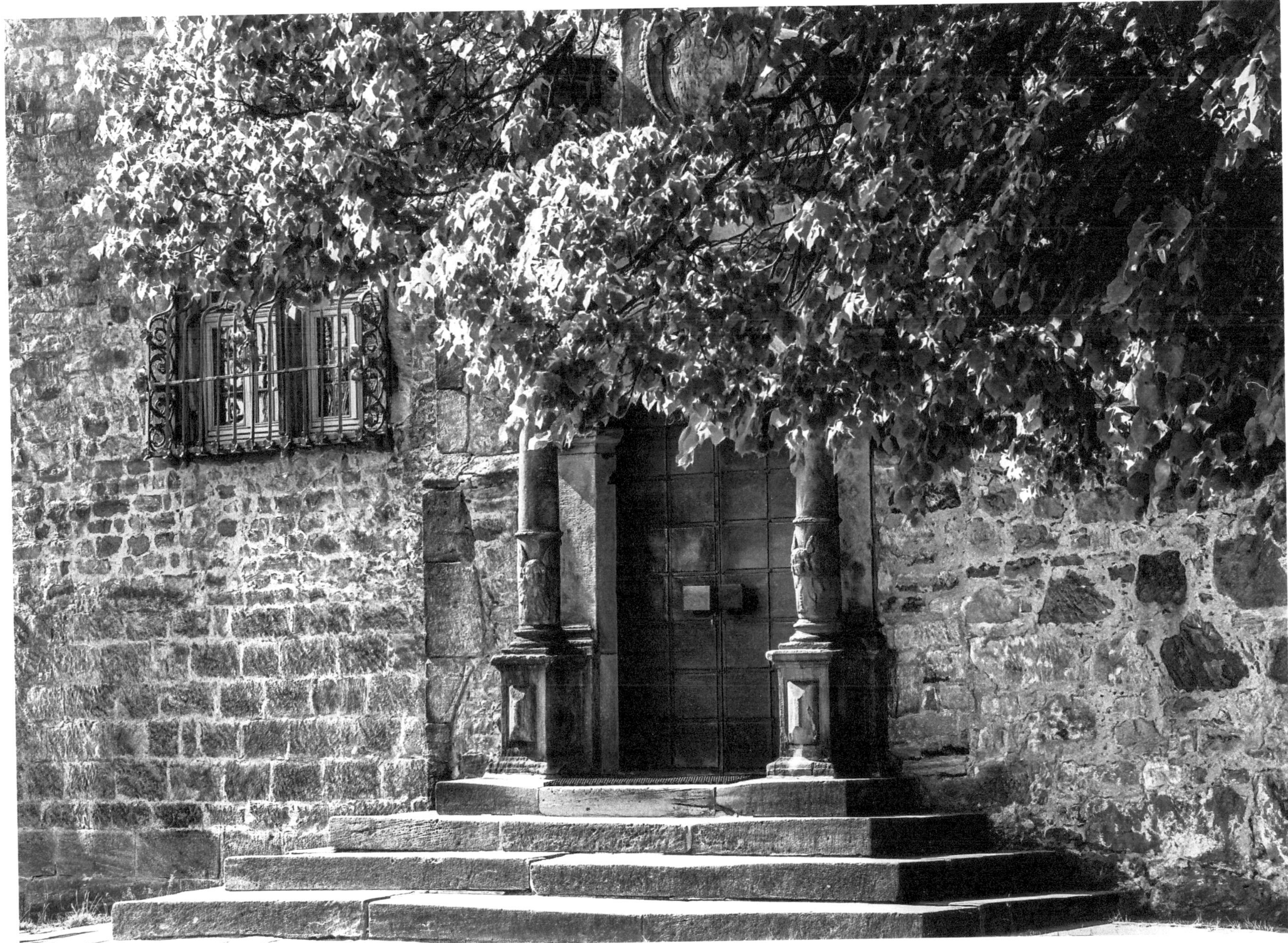

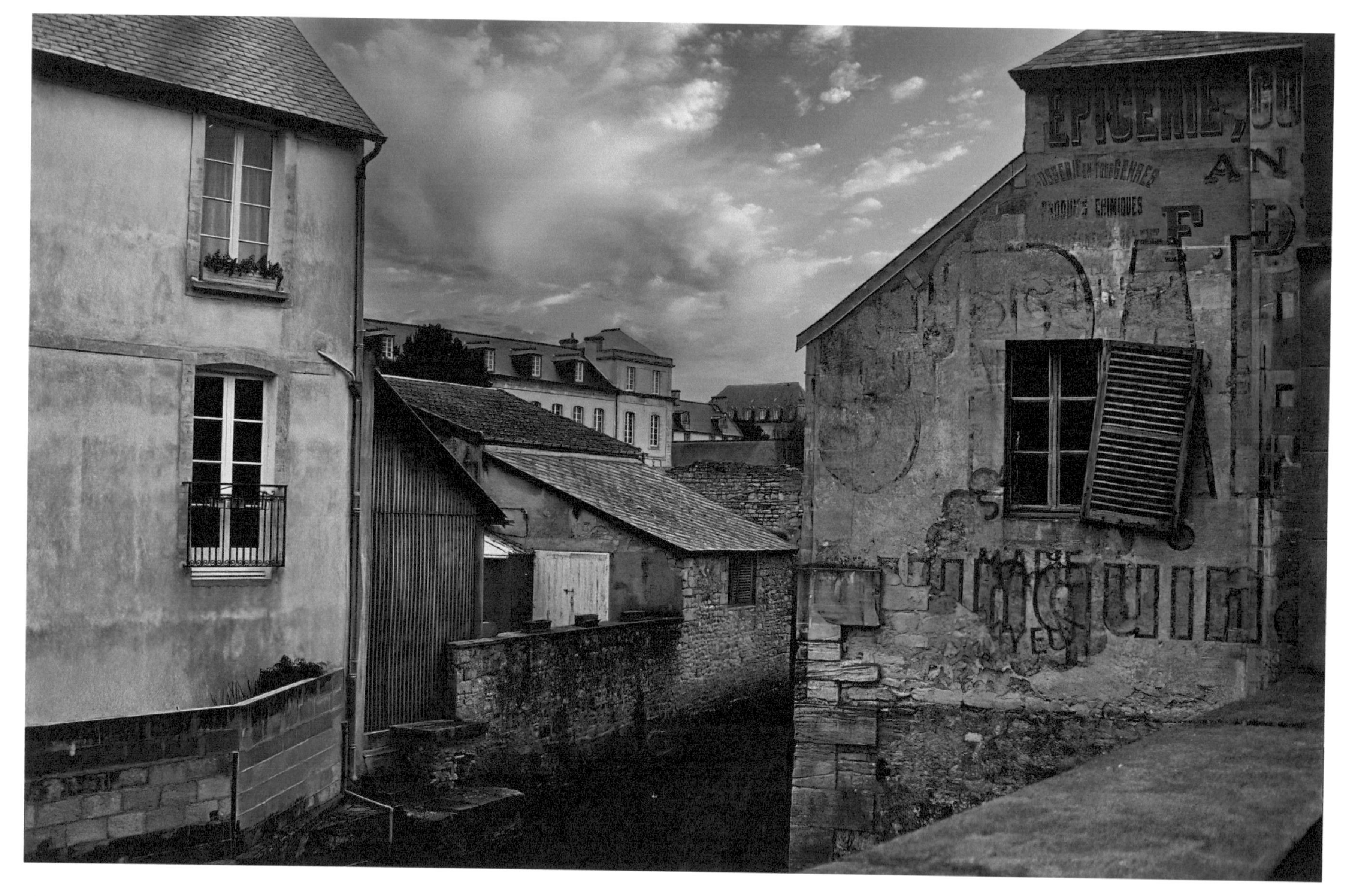

Bayeux is a commune in the Calvados department in Normandy in northwestern France. It lies on the Aure River, northwest of Caen.

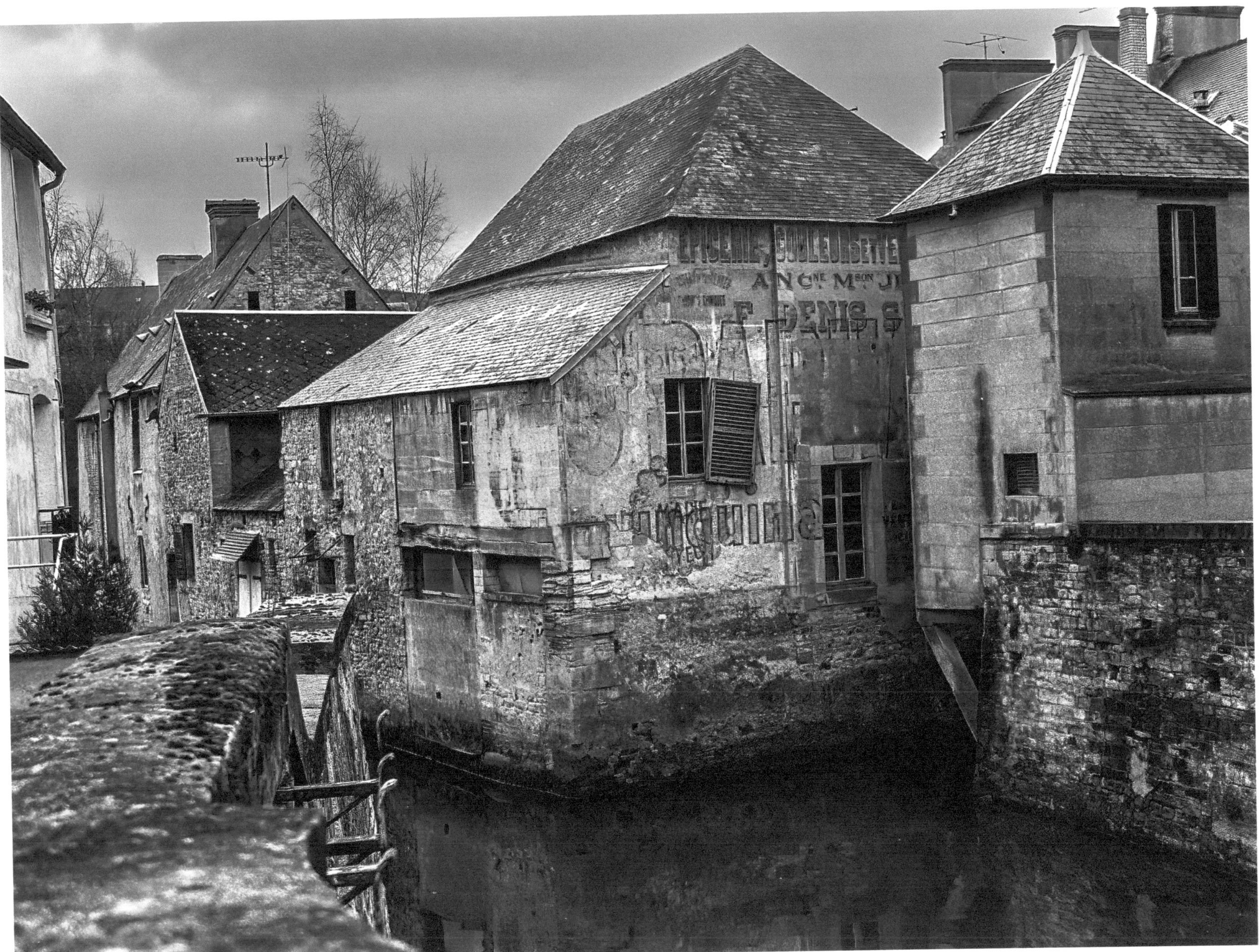
EPICERIE, QUBLEURDETTE
ANG.ne M.on JI
F. DENIS, S

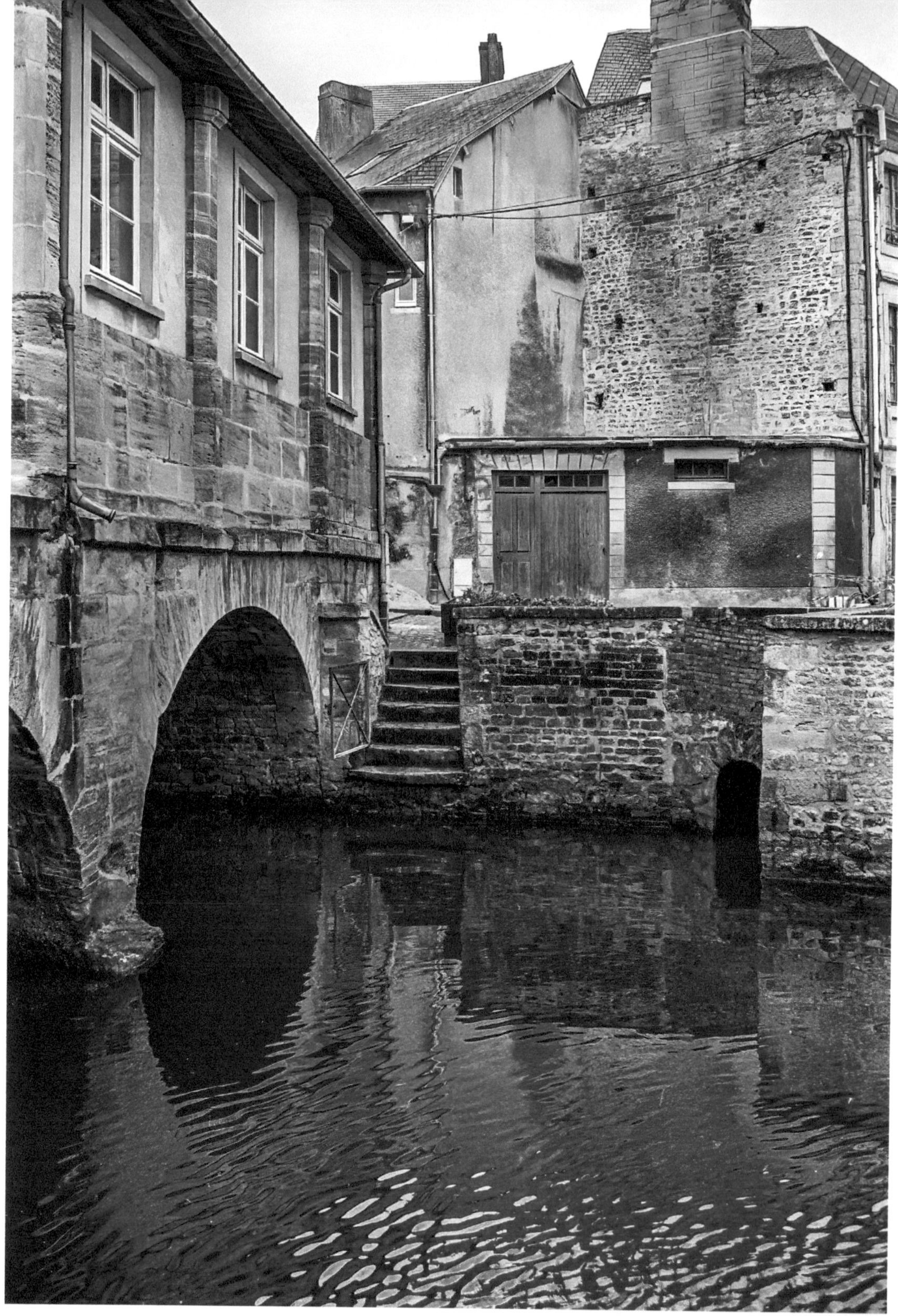

The beauty of imperfection resides in its ability to reveal the authenticity and uniqueness that lies within each of us. It is through embracing our flaws and celebrating our quirks that we find true beauty, for it is in our imperfections that our humanity shines brightest.

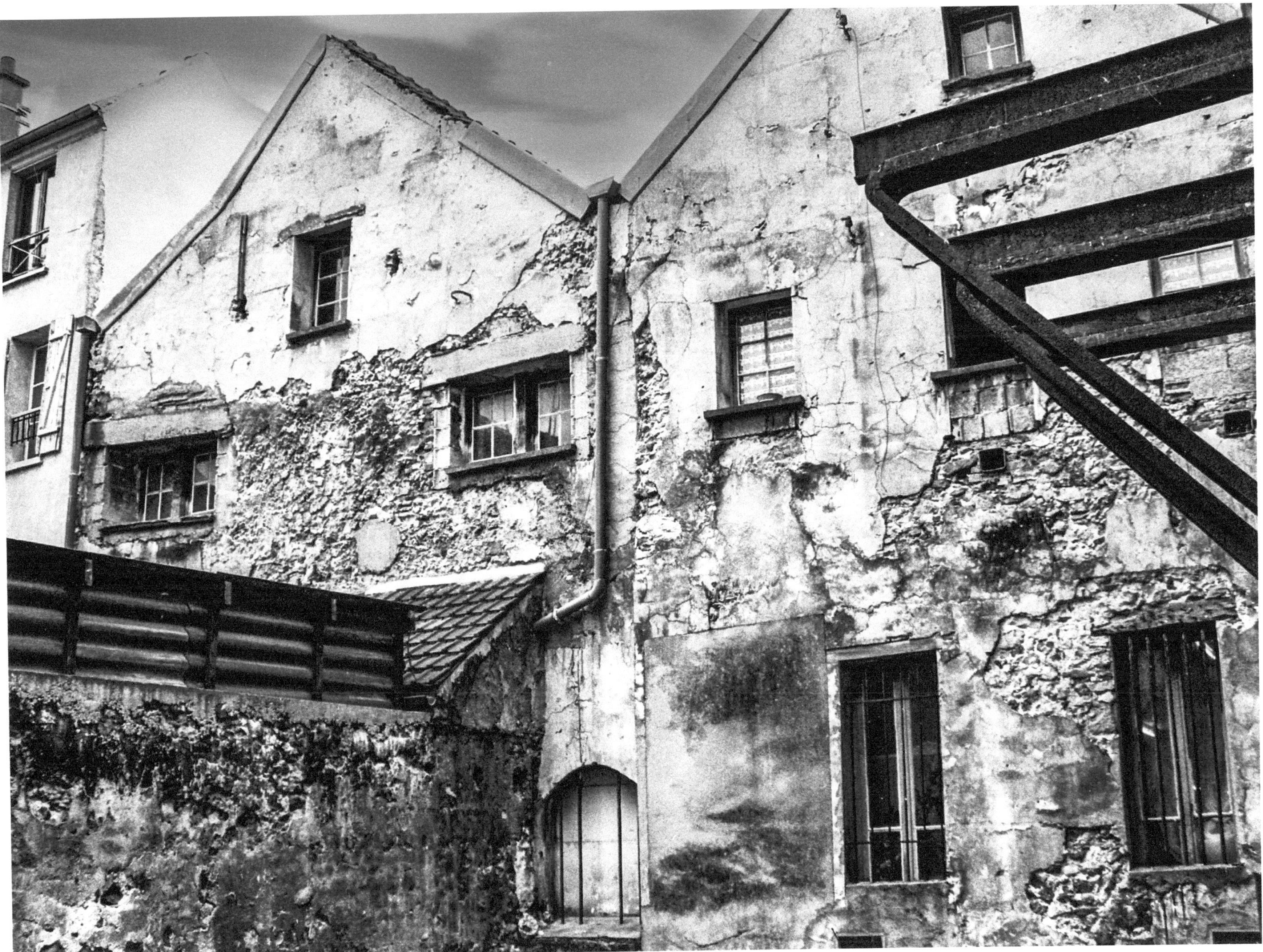

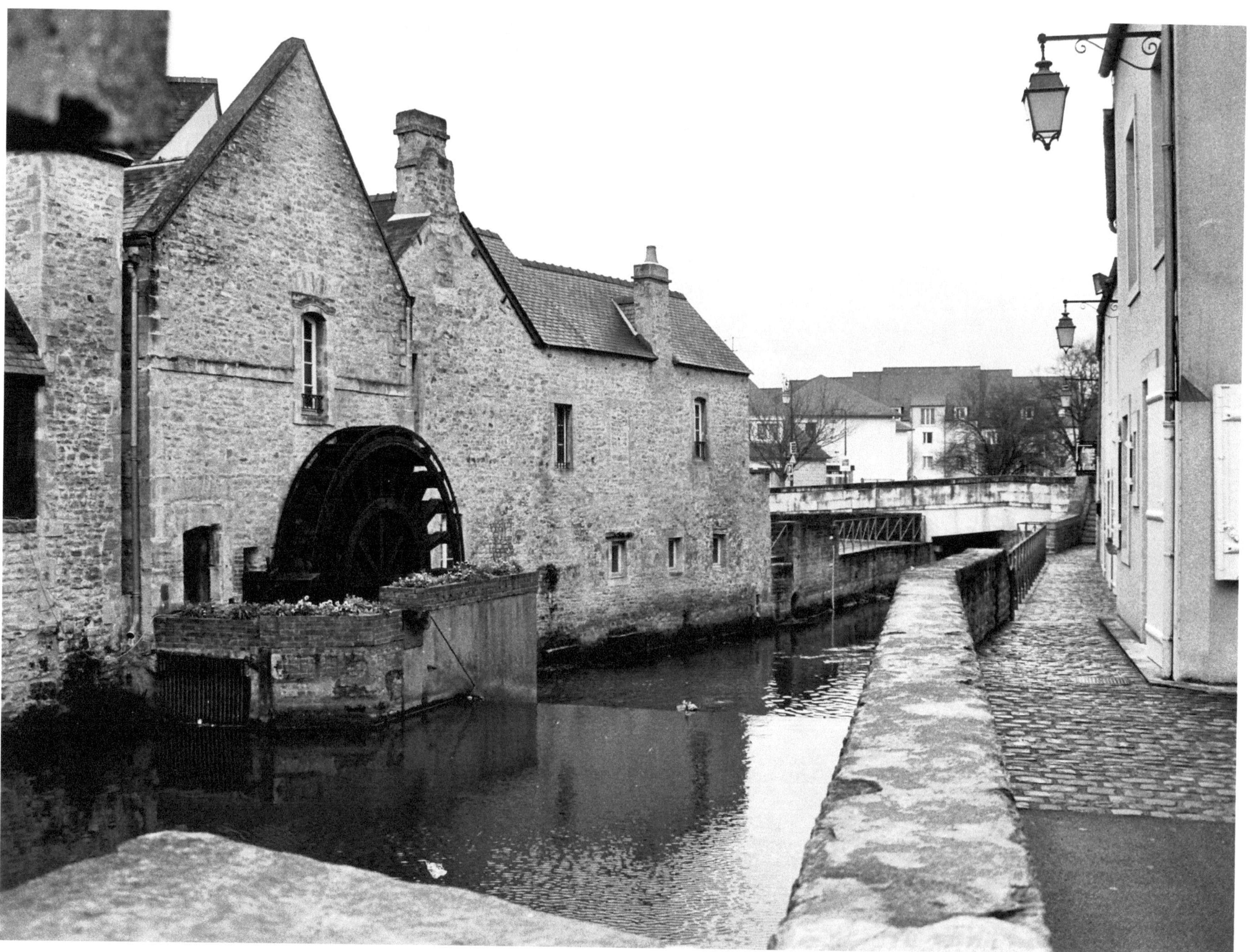

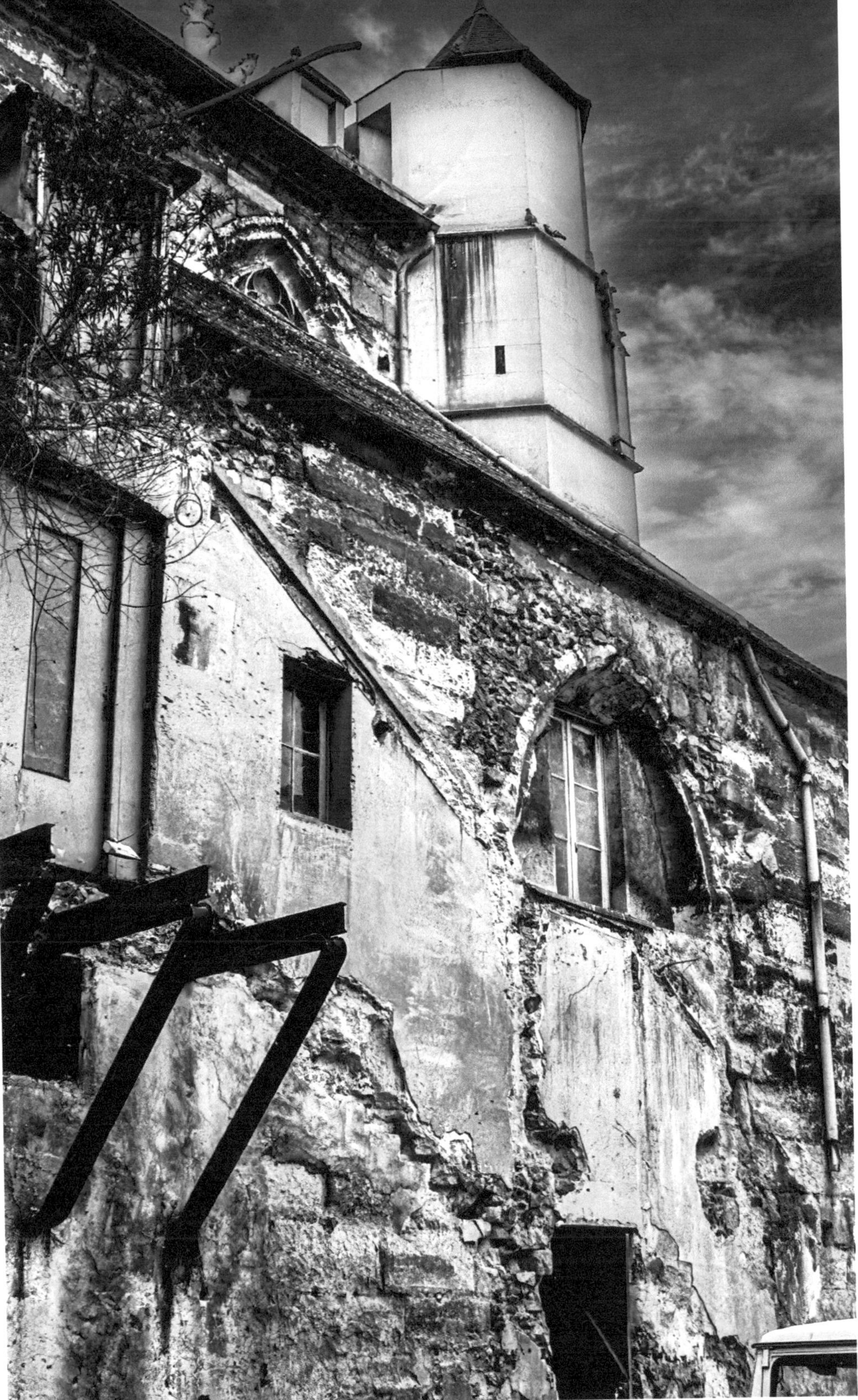

How is there beauty in imperfection?

The concept of beauty in imperfection, also known as wabi-sabi, is rooted in Japanese aesthetics and philosophy. It celebrates the beauty of imperfect, impermanent, and incomplete things. The idea is that imperfection adds character and uniqueness to things, making them more interesting and beautiful. It also encourages acceptance of the natural cycle of growth, decay, and death.

"No human face is exactly the same in its lines on each side, no leaf perfect in its lobes, no branch in its symmetry. All admit irregularity as they imply change, and to banish imperfection is to destroy expression, to check exertion, and paralyze vitality. All things are literally better, lovelier, and more beloved for the imperfections which have been divinely appointed, that the law of human life may be Effort, and the law of human judgment, Mercy."

-John Ruskin (1819-1900), English writer, philosopher, art critic, and polymath of the Victorian era

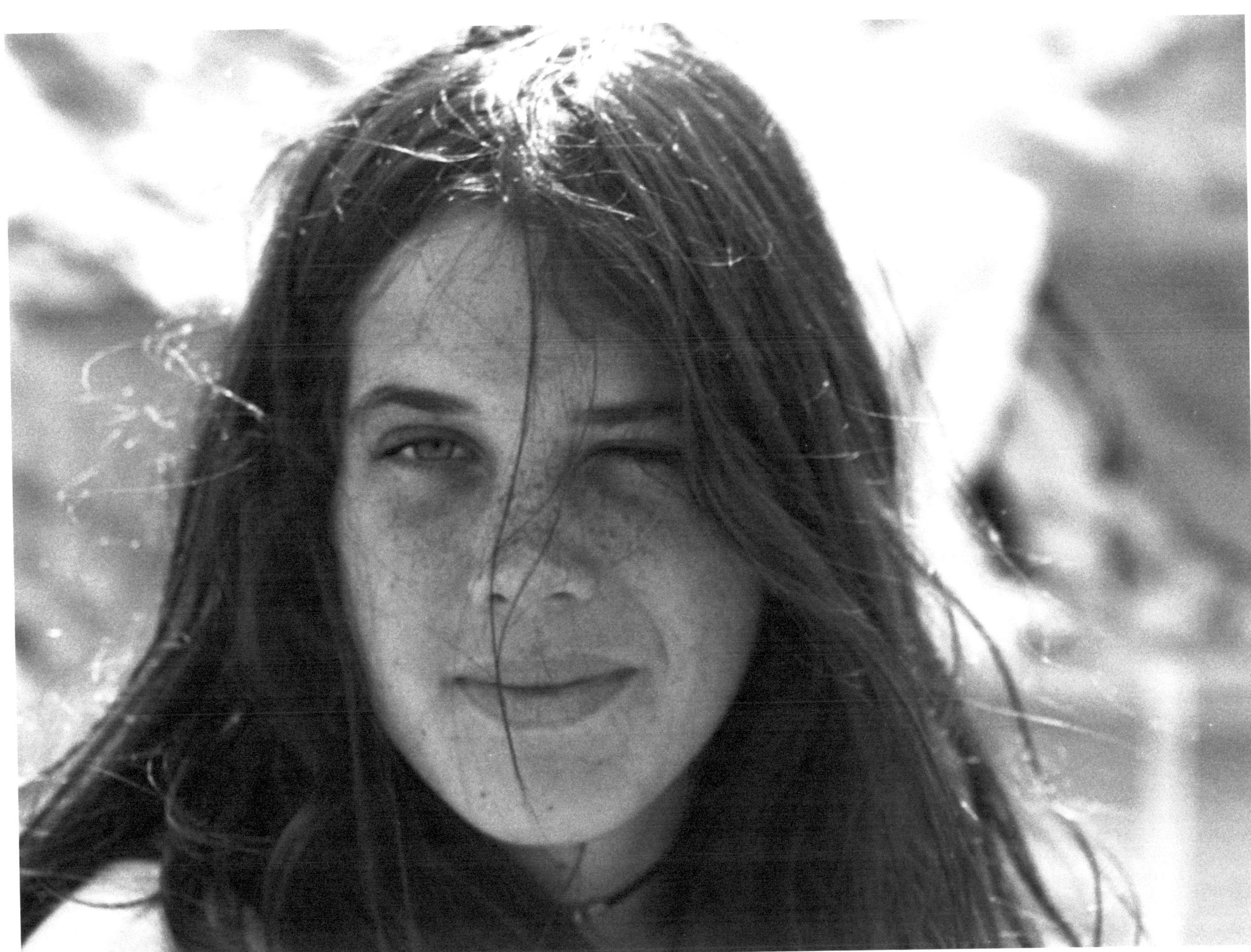

"**True beauty is born through our actions and aspirations and in the kindness, we offer to others.**"
-Alek Wek (1977), South Sudanese-
British model and designer

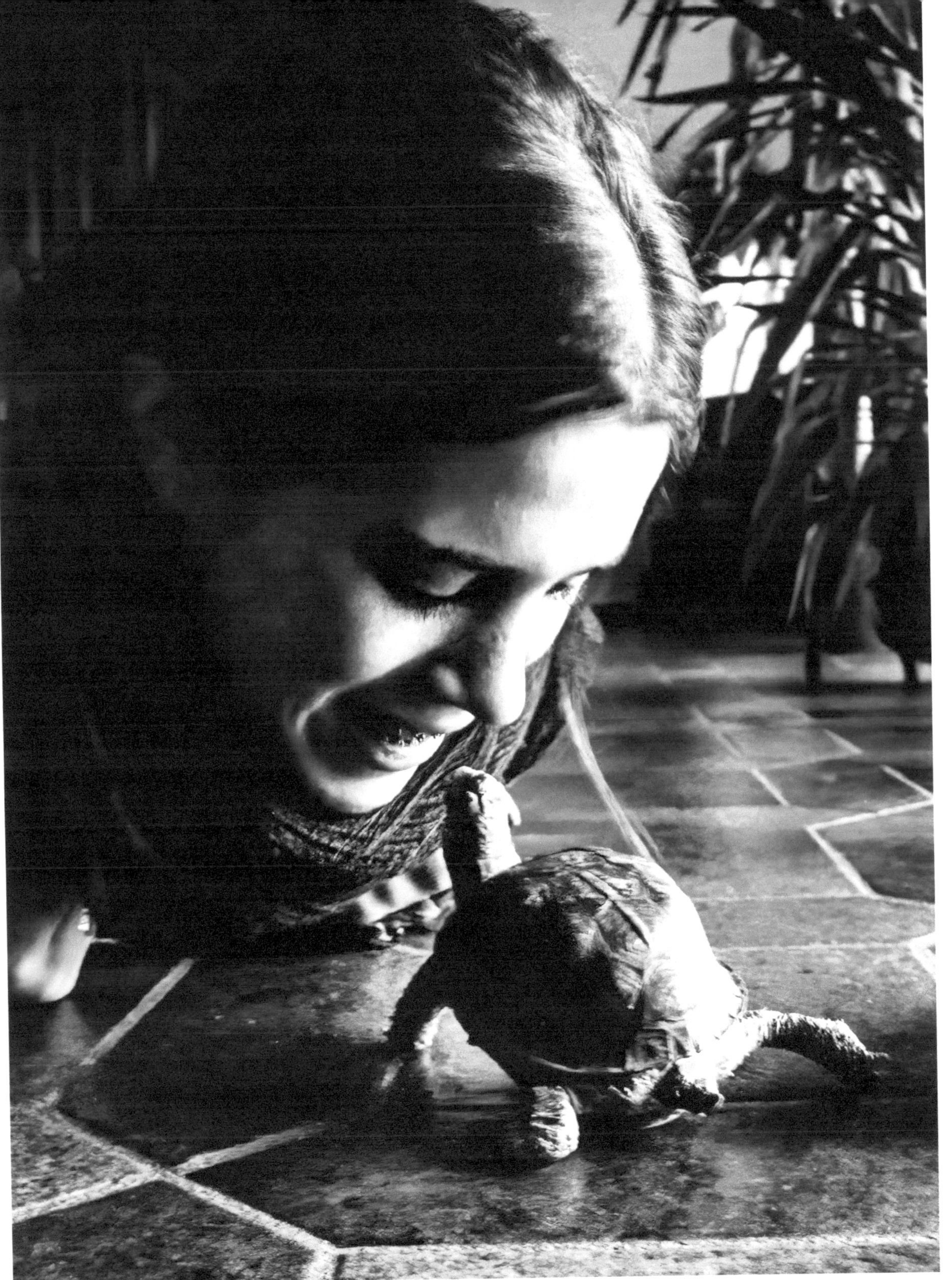

Acknowledgments

It's common to compare ourselves and our work with others, especially in this current age of social media, where everyone's highlight reels are on display. However, being the late bloomer that I am, I've finally realized that real beauty is truly subjective and can be perceived differently by each individual. What one person sees as beautiful, another may not.

This realization has freed me as a photographer because it allowed me to focus on capturing what speaks to me rather than trying to conform to any particular standard or expectation. It has also allowed me to appreciate and celebrate the diversity of my perspectives and interpretations that exist in our world.

Instead of comparing yourself to others, try to focus on honing your craft and developing your own voice and style. Take inspiration from others, but don't let their work define yours. And remember, your perception and interpretation of beauty are just as valid as anyone else's.

I am beyond grateful to the following people for helping me find my way to this very moment. You do make me smile!

I must start with my husband, Bill (again). Without his support, I don't know where I would be as a person or photographer. He respectfully gave me the freedom to grow into who I am today. Sometimes while traveling, I would yell "stop," and he never questioned me except a few times when we were on the Autobahn. Being a designer, he would say, "Hey, you should check it out from this angle," and he was always right. We're both Army brats, so staying in one place can be difficult. However, moving to Europe was our happy place, and though we lived in France for only 12.5 years, it was pure magic. That experience was something I am forever grateful for. Thank you!

My parents, of course. My dad always said, "You must work hard to get ahead in this life." But being who I am, I did not listen. All these years later, I wish I had heard with my heart and paid more attention instead of thinking I knew better. But I'm here in this moment remembering him always telling me how proud he was of me. He was my hero, and I miss him every day.

My brother, Chuck (happily retired family man). We've certainly had our moments, but I'm so proud that no matter what's going on at the time, you have my back as I have yours. You've made me cry, but you've also made me do that ugly belly laugh where the milk sprays out of my nose. Fun Times! LUM!

Aude, Je t'aime. Tu es toujours dans mon cœur!

Katarina Rogers, you remain one of the most beautiful people I know.

"I always find beauty in things that are odd and imperfect – they are much more interesting."
-Marc Jacobs (1963), American fashion designer

Pamela (Pam) Winter is my amazing photo editor and dear friend. You can see her gorgeous photography here:
https://www.viewbug.com/member/pamelawinter
https://fineartamerica.com/profiles/pamela-winter
https://www.pictorem.com/profile/Pamela.Winter

Sal, Heather, Nic, Danny, Edith, Randall, Brigitte, Robert, and Laila: I am so grateful you're a part of my life. I love you, and laughing with you makes everything better!

We hope you have enjoyed viewing some of Cathy's favorite photographs. Through her travels abroad, she has captured and amassed quite a collection of her memories. In addition, she honed her skills over the years by attending many photography classes and seminars related to this art form.

As is typical with most photographers, Cathy stored box after box of moments frozen in time through her photographs. These beautiful images were put away and nearly forgotten.

Cathy never gave up wanting to share some of her favorite photos; finally, she has achieved this goal.

This has inspired Cathy to dig deeper into her vast collection and assemble another publication to share with you.

As fans of her art, we are anxious to see the next edition of many more to come!

Sincerely, her very proud brother, Chuck Waite.